Jump Start Your Career
in Technology & IT
in about 100 Pages

Table of Contents

Let's Start !

Introduction

We all come to that point in our lives when we wish the Calculator app in our favorite operating system had just a little more functionality. Those of weaker resolve turn to surrogates such as Excel, but true believers know that the only tool that befits a mathematician (or just somebody that wants to plot some three-dimensional graphs) is a proper computer algebra system (CAS).

The fields of CAS are full of different tools, from those with aesthetically pleasing front-ends to those whose terseness and Spartan presentation rival that of Notepad. MATLAB is one such tool, serving the more coding-oriented crowds who see mathematics as an extension of the programming discipline. MATLAB stands for MATrix LABoratory, its name being a hint for what it's good at.

For those of you with less experience in these matters, a CAS is essentially very similar to a typical programming language/IDE combination, the difference being that it is oriented towards computation, optimization, and other advanced mathematical things that a programming language often cannot provide. As a result, a CAS typically uses an interpreted, rather than compiled, language. It also brings a wealth of library functions for various problem domains (mathematics, statistics, econometrics, and so on) as well as tools to render graphs, for example.

MATLAB happens to be a highly modular system. What this means is that instead of just getting one application, you get the core MATLAB installation and then purchase one or more toolboxes depending on what your needs are. These toolboxes, broadly speaking, fall into three categories:

- **Scientific** toolboxes related to mathematics, statistics, and optimization. These might include, for example, the Symbolic Math Toolbox that supports things such as symbolic differentiation, or the Statistics Toolbox that gives you—you guessed it—various statistical functions and tools.
- Toolboxes related to specific **problem domains or industries**, such as Aerospace, Econometrics, or the Image Processing Toolbox.
- Toolboxes related specifically to **computation** (i.e. the ways in which calculations are performed), such as the Parallel Computing Toolbox or MATLAB Coder.
- **SIMULINK**, a graphical programming language used for modeling and simulation. SIMULINK is tightly integrated with MATLAB.

What's in This Book

This book covers the core features of MATLAB, including basic language constructs, matrix manipulation, and data visualization. One core functionality that this book does **not** cover is the creation of GUI apps; this is more of a visual topic and is best served with the documentation and samples that MATLAB itself provides.

I will mention various toolboxes from time to time but, to be fair, some of these deserve entire books of their own, and, as Fermat said, "There is not enough space in this margin."

Running MATLAB

MATLAB is typically versioned with a year-letter scheme, so for example, the R2013a release number (this is the revision used for this book) indicates that the release happened in the first half of 2013. MATLAB is available on many platforms, including desktop/laptop platforms (Windows, Mac, and Linux) as well as mobile platforms (Android and iOS).

Mobile versions of MATLAB are not standalone, though—instead, these apps connect either to your desktop MATLAB installation or to the MathWorks Cloud.

To connect a mobile client to a desktop installation, you need to use a special tool called the MATLAB Connector (free to download). The machine must be available on the network, and an instance of MATLAB must be running, and so should the Connector.

MathWorks also provides an alternative connection point for mobile clients called the MathWorks Cloud. Essentially, instead of connecting to your own machine, you connect to a machine hosted by MathWorks, in its own cloud. This requires you to provide your account credentials when connecting, and is useful in cases when you're away from your "native" MATLAB installation but you still need to get some calculations done.

Whichever mobile option you choose, your facilities are limited compared to a proper desktop installation. You get the command window editor (no file editor) and the ability to perform calculations, render graphs, and save them on your mobile device, and that's about it. You miss comprehensive help, the ability to work with scripts, and many other features.

Parallel Computing

If you take MATLAB without any toolboxes, it is not going to support your sophisticated computer infrastructure, and you will have no capabilities for improving performance by parallelizing loops or using clusters of machines.

This is what the Parallel Computing toolbox is for. This toolbox does two things. First, it lets you write code to support parallel computation, allowing you to take advantage of all the cores available on your local machine with a CUDA-capable GPU or to leverage the power of a whole cluster of machines. The other benefit of the toolbox is that other toolboxes now get the ability to leverage the capability of your parallel architectures to perform computations faster.

When it comes to clusters, though, you need another product called the MATLAB Distributed Computing Server (MDCS). This is the server platform that you need to perform computations on clusters of machines and, just like with the multi-core setting, existing toolboxes get the ability to leverage the cluster's resources for purposes of distributed computation. Note that to take advantage of MDCS you also need to install the Parallel Computing toolbox.

Program Deployment

Once you have perfected your calculations, you might want to run them on production systems. In this case, MATLAB has a comprehensive set of toolboxes for various integration options depending on your preferred style of interaction with the outside world. Here are your choices:

- **MATLAB Compiler** lets you compile and run applications written entirely in MATLAB. Note that part of MATLAB's infrastructure is its ability to build user interfaces, so you're not restricted to command-line apps. This allows calculations to be performed on any platform without having to install MATLAB. Keep in mind that the performance of the code will not exceed that of the Desktop MATLAB installation.
- **MATLAB Builder** lets you wrap your MATLAB code as a .NET, COM, or Java component or as an Excel add-in. This way, you can keep using your favorite programming languages while interfacing with the component wrappers when necessary.
- **Spreadsheet Link** lets you link from Excel to MATLAB. This allows you, for example, to access MATLAB's variables right in Excel.
- **MATLAB Coder** is a package that lets you convert MATLAB code directly into C code. This allows you to compile and run code as part of an ordinary C application on any platform, including platforms that are not supported by MATLAB itself.

When it comes to computational performance, with MATLAB your results may vary. When using fine-tuned, optimized algorithms, your code can be as fast as if you wrote it using C++ (or indeed faster if you leverage, e.g., the Parallel Toolbox). In many cases, however, particularly when working with MATLAB's object model, you may end up experiencing performance that is significantly inferior to what one would achieve using a modern compiled programming language. As with all things, it is best to check your particular calculations and port if necessary.

MATLAB Variants

MATLAB is a commercial product. Other, free-to-use systems exist out there that offer similar facilities to MATLAB (at least with regards to the core installation) and a syntax that is, for the most part, MATLAB-compatible. Two such systems are SciLab and GNU Octave.

Most of the examples in this book are compatible with said systems, except for when certain particular toolboxes are used. It's worth noting, however, that in certain cases the syntax does diverge slightly—for example, MATLAB generates normally distributed numbers with **randn**, whereas SciLab uses **rand** with an additional **n** parameter.

Discrepancies between different MATLAB-compatible implementations are too numerous to mention and would distract the readers of this book. Thus, while this book uses MATLAB syntax exclusively, the vast majority of the examples should run just fine on Octave (which aims to be fully MATLAB-compliant) and similar systems (such as SciLab). If something goes wrong, just check the documentation for adjustments that need to be made to get the code running

Off We Go!

Before we set off on our adventure, there's one point I want to make. When mathematicians fail to label their graphs, they can typically expect anything from a slap on the wrist to a reduced grade. I've also been guilty of this crime in preparation of this manuscript, but with good reason: the quality of MATLAB's axis, legend, and title rendering leaves a lot to be desired, especially when rendered to image format. This will hopefully improve in the future.

Alright, enough talk. Fire up MATLAB and let's start exploring!

Chapter 1 User Interface

Showing user interface screenshots in a book may not be the best idea, but to MATLAB's credit, it does have a rather well-designed interface that makes certain common operations simpler. Plus, we need to agree on the notation regarding the windows and controls. So let's get through this quickly, shall we?

Windows

When you open MATLAB for the first time, you're likely to see something like this:

Figure 1: MATLAB, in the flesh. With luck, you will spend days, I mean, years in this window.

Well, maybe without the file editor, but I've added it just in case. What you're looking at is a highly modular (there's that word again) system of windows: effectively, everything except the top-level ribbon toolbar is a separate window that can be detached and moved to a different part of the container window or even a different monitor.

Let us discuss the different windows that make up the default MATLAB window layout. They are:

- **Command Window**: This is essentially a console where you can type in commands for immediate execution. Type in **2+2** and you get **4**, type in **foo** and MATLAB will go off looking for a variable called **foo** or, failing that, for a script **foo.m** on the available paths. (More about paths later.)

- **Editor**: This is where scripts can be edited. The Editor window has a tabbed interface, but you can "detach" any of the tabs to a separate window. The Editor window also adds a few ribbon tabs, namely Editor, Publish, and View. We'll talk about those in the chapter on scripts.

- **Workspace**: This is a list of all the variables currently being used. In addition to showing variable names and (where possible) values, you can also tell MATLAB to display some basic statistical properties of arrays:

Figure 2: Picking columns for the Workspace window. For arrays, you can display statistical results such as average, variance, or standard deviation values.

- **Command History**: This window contains a list of all the previous commands you've executed. This is, arguably, the least useful window due to the fact that recent commands are rarely needed, and when they are, you can simply press the up/down arrow keys on the keyboard to cycle through the previously entered commands.

- **Current Folder**: This window, together with the toolbar just above it, lets you navigate, open, and execute scripts from a particular folder. The window menu (opened by pressing the downward-pointing arrow) also has various file-related commands (e.g., commands to create new files or folders). The selected folder is automatically added to MATLAB's path settings, so executing a script by name from this folder will work, whereas when you're accessing scripts from other folders, they have to be on the MATLAB path. Also, for files currently selected in the current folder, you might see a preview window below that shows internals of the file. For example, for MAT files, this window shows the value of the stored variables.

- **Ribbon:** This is the part that contains all the controls. The ribbon interface is a relatively new addition to MATLAB, with earlier versions having an ordinary toolbar instead.

- **Quick-Access Bar:** This is a special toolbar that appears in the top-right corner of the screen. It's a place where you can add the most frequently used commands that will never be obscured, unlike the Ribbon interface, where only one tab may be visible at any time.

The Paths of MATLAB

If you go ahead and type `cruller` into the command window (regardless of what the current path is), you're likely to see something like this:

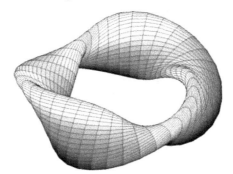

Figure 3: A cruller—apparently a type of fried pastry.

The above shape is generated by one of MATLAB's sample scripts, and the reason you got it is because the file that renders it, `cruller.m`, happens to reside in a location that is added to MATLAB's execution path by default.

Essentially, to make use of any files in MATLAB, those files need to be placed on MATLAB's path. To configure these paths, look for the Set Path button of the Home path of the ribbon. Click **Set Path** to open up the **Set Path** window:

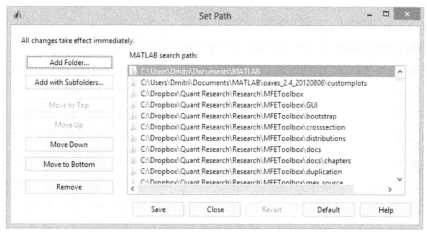

Figure 4: Set Path window.

The Set Path window lets you add a folder (or a folder with all its subfolders included) that will subsequently be used for searching for scripts to execute. You can also move the list elements up and down to indicate search priority (higher path position means higher priority).

Shortcuts

If you find yourself writing the same command over and over again, you might want to turn it into a shortcut to be placed either in the Quick Access Bar just to the left of the Search Documentation box or on a separate toolstrip tab called Shortcuts. Shortcuts can be created either via the Context menu in the Command History window (see, it's not entirely useless!) or by pressing the New Shortcut button on the top-level toolbar.

The Shortcut Editor is fairly simple: it lets you label your shortcut and decide where you want it to be placed, and with what icon:

Figure 5: Shortcut Editor window

Help and Documentation

MATLAB has a rather elaborate help system, so let's examine its different facets.

The simplest way to get to MATLAB's documentation is to press the **Help** button (or **F1**). This opens up the documentation browser that includes documentation for all the products (i.e. toolboxes) that you have installed. It also lets you search for specific topics, with reasonably fast completion, too!

Figure 6: Help window

In terms of search, similar functionality is available in the Search Documentation text box in the top-right corner of the page: simply start typing and MATLAB will try to guess what it is you're looking for.

If you need information on a particular function, you can use yet another tool called the Function Browser. This is the equivalent of the full documentation that is shown in a pop-up window instead.

The simplest way of bringing up the function browser is to press the fx button that's just to the left of the input line on the command window. This gives a tree-like listing of all the functions. When you click a function, you get a documentation popup on the right:

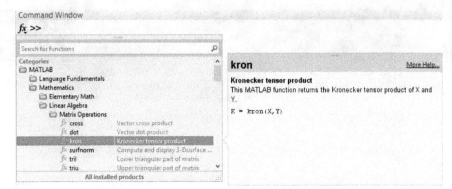

Figure 7: Function browser drill-down window with documentation preview.

If you already know the function name, getting documentation for that function is even easier: simply press **F1** when on a function and you get the documentation pop-up for that function:

```
>> blsprice
```

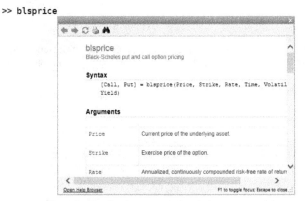

Figure 8: Function browser pop-up window.

The pop-up is simply the ordinary documentation browser packaged in a pop-up window; you can easily move between it and the command window or open the full-frame documentation browser if required.

But that's not all! You can also get help on a particular function in plain text by typing its name prefixed by the word **help** into the command window:

```
>> help cross
 cross  Vector cross product.
    C = cross(A,B) returns the cross product of the vectors
```

```
A and B.   That is, C = A x B.   A and B must be 3 element
vectors.

C = cross(A,B) returns the cross product of A and B along the
first dimension of length 3.
```

This may not be the most convenient way of reading documentation, but the option is here if you need it, e.g., if you need to work in MATLAB purely in terminal mode (because we all know how atrociously slow running X11 over VPN is).

If you know only part of an identifier, you can use **lookfor** to perform a search. For example, here's a search for all the Black Scholes-related functions (note some spurious results below):

```
>> lookfor bls
blsdelta                   - Black-Scholes sensitivity to underlying price
change.
blsgamma                   - Black-Scholes sensitivity to underlying delta
change.
blsimpv                    - Black-Scholes implied volatility.
blslambda                  - Black-Scholes elasticity.
blsprice                   - Black-Scholes put and call option pricing.
blsrho                     - Black-Scholes sensitivity to interest rate change.
blstheta                   - Black-Scholes sensitivity to time until maturity
change.
blsvega                    - Black-Scholes sensitivity to underlying price
volatility.
blscheck                   - Black-Scholes input argument checking.
blspriceeng                - Engine function for Black-Scholes option pricing
model.
converttobls               - Convert BLS parameters to the domain used by the
lower-level
wblstat                    - Mean and variance of the Weibull distribution.
tablseq                    - Equality table for lifting schemes.
```

Another way MATLAB helps you use functions is by highlighting the parameter you are currently entering in a small overlay window. This also has a **More Help...** link, which opens a documentation browser.

```
>> blsprice(100, 110
```

Figure 9: Parameter help as you type.

In addition to local documentation, MATLAB's documentation is also available online at http://www.mathworks.com/help/matlab/.

Introspection

To find out what toolboxes you've actually got installed, simply type **ver** into the **Command Window**. This will give you a listing of every single installed product and its version.

Also, keep in mind that some toolboxes supply their own apps—these are essentially separate GUI-based applications that integrate with MATLAB. These are available on the Apps tab:

When in Trouble...

If you have trouble with something in MATLAB, your first port of call should be the menu item under **Help | Request Support**. This lets you file a support request without leaving MATLAB. As you may have guessed, it does require your MathWorks credentials (the same ones you used to download MATLAB in the first place).

Then there is plenty of community support. StackOverflow is an obvious choice (unlike Mathematica, its lack of a front-end prevented it from getting its own StackExchange site), and so is MATLAB Central—a special website for all things MATLAB. This website includes a section for sharing downloadable scripts and extensions (File Exchange), its own Q&A section (Answers), a Newsgroup for general discussion, a Blogs section, and Cody—a game that challenges programmers and helps them expand their knowledge of MATLAB.

If all else fails, just type **why** into the console window and press **Enter**. MATLAB will attempt to explain to you just why things aren't going the way they should be. Beware though, because in the majority of cases, MATLAB tries to blame some mythical co-worker that you might not even have!

Chapter 2 Data Types

We are going to begin our relationship with MATLAB by looking at the different numeric types that MATLAB supports. We will also discuss some of the predefined constants that are available to users when working with numeric data, and then we will then discuss the various formats in which numeric data can be printed in the command window. Subsequently, we shall discuss character strings—these are not as important as numbers, but they are still used in many places within MATLAB. We will then look at structures, which provide a great way of effortlessly grouping related data together. Finally, we will talk about the more obscure concept of cell arrays, and finish the chapter off with a discussion of function handles.

One thing I would like to point out here is that an in-depth discussion of arrays and matrices is postponed, because I am going to dedicate a whole chapter to them. However, I will briefly mention arrays in this chapter.

Numeric Types

MATLAB supports various data types, and of most importance to us are obviously the numeric types, i.e. data types used to store numbers. In MATLAB's terminology, a data type is called a *class*, but to avoid confusing those of my readers who are already practicing programmers, I will keep using the term *data type* whenever I can.

There are two ways of getting the class, or the data type, of something. The first is to use the `class` function, which yields just the data type.

```
>> x=5; class(x)

ans =
double
```

The semicolon in this example is used to separate two statements on a single line, and also suppresses the output from the first statement (x=5). Don't worry, we'll explain it all a bit later.

Alternatively, you can get even more info by using the **whos** command. This command lists not just the type of the variable but also its name, size, and other attributes:

```
>> whos x

  Name      Size            Bytes  Class     Attributes
  x         1x1                 8  double
```

So the first thing to note is that the default data type for numeric values in MATLAB is double-precision. We can verify this by using the **class** function. For example, if we type **class(5)** we get a result of **double**. If we want single-precision instead, we can use the **single** function:

```
>> y = single(5); class(y)
ans =
single
```

But what does single and double precision mean? Well, essentially, it means that both of these types can store real numbers, i.e. numbers with whole and fractional parts, and the difference between single and double is how much memory they take.

```
>> whos x, whos y

  Name      Size            Bytes  Class     Attributes
  x         1x1                 8  double
  Name      Size            Bytes  Class     Attributes
  y         1x1                 4  single
```

As you can see, the double-precision number takes up twice as many bytes (8 as opposed to 4 for a single-precision number), so it can store larger values or values with higher precision. For example, here's how the representation of π varies depending on data type:

```
>> single(pi)
ans =
        3.141593
>> pi
ans =
            3.14159265358979
```

If you want to know the limits of those values, you can use the **realmin** and **realmax** functions to figure out the minimum and maximum values that can be stored.

```
>> realmin('single'), realmax('double')

ans =
  1.1755e-38
ans =
  1.7977e+308
```

MATLAB also supports integer data types, i.e. data types which only contain a whole part of the number. For example, if you load an image, each pixel of an image might have red, green, and blue values ranging from 0 to 255. If you need to define integers yourself, conversions are made using the `int` and `uint` functions for signed and unsigned integers respectively. Each function is postfixed by the number of bits, so for example, to get a 64-bit unsigned integer with a value of 5 you can write:

```
>> z = uint64(5), whos z

z =

              5
  Name      Size            Bytes  Class      Attributes
  z         1x1                 8  uint64
```

Both signed and unsigned integers are available in 8, 16, 32, and 64-bit precision.

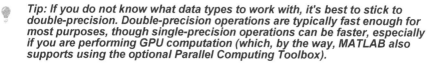 *Tip: If you do not know what data types to work with, it's best to stick to double-precision. Double-precision operations are typically fast enough for most purposes, though single-precision operations can be faster, especially if you are performing GPU computation (which, by the way, MATLAB also supports using the optional Parallel Computing Toolbox).*

Inf, NaN and Other Constants

If we divide 1 by 0, we get infinity, which is represented in MATLAB with the `inf` constant. You can use `inf` in your own calculations, for example in symbolic calculations where you calculate the limit when something goes to infinity. You can use the `isinf` function to test if something is equal to infinity.

`inf` is an example of a predefined MATLAB constant. There aren't many such constants in MATLAB, but there are a few that we need to discuss.

Apart from `inf`, there is `nan`, short for "not a number." This constant represents a value that is neither real nor complex. Expressions such as `inf/inf`, `0/0` or any arithmetic expressions involving a `nan` yield a `nan`. You can use the `isnan` function to test for this. Note that, unlike `inf`, you cannot test for a `nan` using comparison operators: both `==` and `~=` will yield `false`.

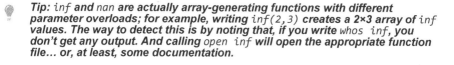 *Tip: `inf` and `nan` are actually array-generating functions with different parameter overloads; for example, writing `inf(2,3)` creates a 2×3 array of `inf` values. The way to detect this is by noting that, if you write `whos inf`, you don't get any output. And calling `open inf` will open the appropriate function file... or, at least, some documentation.*

MATLAB has a few other constants. First, there are limit constants for maximum and minimum integers and floating-point numbers. For example, to get the maximum possible integer we can use the **intmax** constant.

Then there are predefined constants such as **pi** and **i/j**. **pi** (π) has a predictable value, 3.14..., but being a constant (rather than a function), it can be redefined—probably not a good idea, though. If you look at the constants **i** and **j** (these are actually functions, so you can declare your own variables with these names), you will see that their representation is somewhat different than what we have seen previously.

```
>> i

ans =
        0       +     1i
```

In fact, doing a **whos** on the result tells us that, while it has a class of **double**, it is also a complex number:

```
>> whos ans

  Name      Size          Bytes  Class      Attributes
  ans       1x1              16  double     complex
```

Unlike a double-precision value, the complex number in this example is a combination of two double-precision values (one real and one imaginary), so the variable takes 16 bytes instead of the usual eight. Note that complex numbers can also use single-precision values instead of double-precision ones. MATLAB's use of complex numbers is pervasive, so if you take a square root of a negative number or try to solve a quadratic equation that has complex roots, MATLAB will give you complex results rather than showing an error:

```
>> sqrt(-2)
ans =
   0.0000 + 1.4142i
```

Finally, MATLAB has the constant **eps**, which represents the relative floating-point accuracy, i.e. the distance to the next largest floating-point value.

Numeric Output Formats

Let us make a sufficiently big number, say 10^{10}:

```
>> 10^10

ans =
   1.0000e+10
```

As you can see in the output, the number is presented using engineering notation. We can customize the way that numbers are output by using the **format** command. For example, to avoid the engineering notation for this number, I can specify the format as **longg**. This lets me see the number fully:

```
>> format longg
>> 10^10

ans =
              10000000000
```

Alternatively, we can tell MATLAB to use the currency format, which leaves only two decimal places. On the other hand, we can, for example, ensure that all numeric values are output in hexadecimal format.

```
>> format bank
>> ans

ans =
 10000000000.00

>> format hex
>> ans

ans =
   4202a05f20000000
```

MATLAB also supports a formatting style that keeps fractions in ratio format, so instead of evaluating the numeric value of a division, it tries to keep the result as a fraction.

```
>> format rat
>> 2*3/7+1/12

ans =
      79/84
```

Note however that this does **not** imply symbolic evaluation, and dividing **pi** by 2 will yield a fraction that is sufficiently close to the real value of **pi** over 2.

```
>> pi/2

ans =
      355/226
```

For a full list of available numeric formats, check out the documentation section of the **format** command. This contains a list of every supported format string that is available in MATLAB. Please note that the format command only affects the representation of a number, and not the value that is actually stored. Just because MATLAB is showing a number to two decimal digits does not mean that the rest of it was suddenly lost. All the information is still there—you just do not see it.

Arrays

We have a whole chapter on the subject of arrays ahead of us so, to keep things brief, here is a small introduction.

Imagine you need to store information about several successive measurements. Sure, you could give each of those measurements its own variable (a, b, c, and so on) but this is rather impractical. Instead, what you can do is to declare an array—a structure specifically designed to store several values. Arrays are declared and initialized with square brackets, for example:

```
>> values = [1 2 3]

values =
     1    2    3
```

To access an element of an array, you put the element's index right after the array name in round brackets. Unlike in some programming languages, array indices start with 1. The round brackets let you both read array elements and change their values:

```
>> values(2)
ans =
     2

>> values(3) = 15
values =
     1    2    15
```

Arrays form the basis of pretty much everything that happens in MATLAB.

Characters and Strings

When it comes to computation, we are mainly concerned with numeric data, but we also sometimes need to use textual data. For this, we use character strings, which are simply arrays of characters.

Strings are defined by delimiting text with single quotation marks:

```
>> s = 'hello'

s =
hello
```

To make a single quote part of a string, you just type it twice:

```
>> 'let''s go'

ans =
let's go
```

Let's use the **whos** command to see what we just made.

```
>> whos ans

  Name      Size            Bytes  Class    Attributes
   ans      1x8                16  char
```

As you can see, a string in our case is simply an array of eight characters. MATLAB uses fixed-length Unicode characters of two bytes each, thus our eight-character string actually takes up 16 bytes of memory.

You can, of course, access individual string characters. For example, to get the first character, you can write **ans(1)**. Note that the data type of the result is still **char**:

```
>> ans(1); class(ans)

ans =
char
```

The simplest way of joining strings together is to simply use square brackets around the parts to join:

```
>> a = 'hello';
>> b = 'world';
>> [a ', ' b '!']

ans =
hello, world!
```

Note however that attempting to include numeric values into the concatenation can lead to unforeseen consequences, such as having your numeric value converted to a character symbol with the corresponding ASCII code.

```
>> s = 'test'

s =
test

>> s(1) + 'a'

ans =
   213
```

The reverse is useful though: for example, to quickly get a line break between two lines of text, you can rely on MATLAB to convert the number 10 into the character code for a line break. Thus, adding a line break between two pieces of text is as simple as:

```
>> ['hello' 10 'world']
ans =
hello
world
```

To get numeric data in text form, simply use the **num2str** function:

```
>> age = 30;
>> ['I am ' num2str(age) ' years old']

ans =
I am 30 years old
```

One place where strings are used is in writing something to the command window. For that, we can use the **disp** function:

```
>> disp(ans)
```

```
I am 30 years old
```

Strings are used in many places. For example, to plot a graph of $\sqrt{x} \cdot \sin x^2$ (we'll talk about plots in detail a little bit later), you can provide the function as a string:

```
>> ezplot('sqrt(x) * sin(x^2)')
```

MATLAB has lots of functions for string manipulation and conversion. For example, you get string comparison functions **strcmp** and **strcmpi** for case-sensitive and insensitive comparisons:

```
>> strcmpi('abc', 'ABC')

ans =
    1
```

In practice, though, you are unlikely to need any of these functions that often.

Structures

Let's say that in our MATLAB program we need to store some data about a person, such as their name and age. We can certainly use two variables for this or, as an alternative, we can define a structure. Here is what it looks like:

```
>> person.name = 'john';
>> person.age = 22

person =
    name: 'john'
     age: 22
```

How is this possible? What does it mean? Well, there's a bit of magic going on here. As you may have noticed already, MATLAB is an environment where you don't need to declare values before assigning values to them. For example, writing **x=2** automatically creates a variable called **x**. The same principle is at play in the above code listing.

The idea is that when we wrote **person.name = 'john'**, we effectively created a structure called **person** and we created a field called **name** in that structure. A structure array can be thought of as a set of values that are addressed using the dot (.) operator. Note that, unlike in a typical programming language, we didn't have to declare the structure beforehand—we just start using it. And it may seem as though **person** is just one entity, but in actual fact, it's an array that has just one element. Here's the proof:

```
>> person(1)

ans =
    name: 'Sherlock'
     age: 60
```

The fields of a structure can be practically anything, and indeed a field can itself be a structure. For example, our structure can have an address field, itself a structure with a house number and street name. We can then assign this address to a person's address.

```
>> address.houseNumber = '221B';
>> address.streetName = 'Baker st.';
>> person.address = address

person =
       name: 'Sherlock'
        age: 60.00
    address: [1x1 struct]
```

And, of course, **person.address** is not just a single structure; it is, as all things in MATLAB, an array of elements. And we can dynamically add another address to the person's address field, for example:

```
>> person.address(2).houseNumber = '8-9';
>> person.address(2).streetName = 'Hyde Park Pl'

person =
       name: 'Sherlock'
        age: 60
    address: [1x2 struct]
```

Cell Arrays

Before we begin talking about cell arrays, there's a critical point that needs to be explained. In MATLAB, strictly speaking, **everything** is an array. To verify that this is so, let's declare a single numeric variable. If we use the **whos** command, we can see the size of the variable listed as **1×1**:

```
>> x=42;
>> whos x

  Name      Size            Bytes  Class     Attributes
```

```
x           1x1                   8  double
```

So even though it appears as a scalar value, it is in fact a 1×1 array. Moreover, because MATLAB can dynamically resize arrays, we can take this **x** and turn it into a 1×2 array just by writing:

```
>> x(2) = 24

x =
     42                  24
```

You can clearly see from the output that **x** has become a 1×2 array.

This brings us to the idea of cell arrays. Essentially, if you consider structures as entities whose fields are addressable via their names, then cell arrays are that same idea, but the elements are kept in an array, and are addressable by position. Let us define that same **person** entity we met previously, but using a cell array instead:

```
>> address = { 123, 'London Road' };
>> person = { 'John', 22, address }

person =
     'John'    [22]    {1x2 cell}
```

As you can see, instead of using named fields, we simply list the elements of a cell array inside curly braces (as opposed to round brackets which are used for ordinary arrays). Now if we do a **whos person** you'll see it defined with a class of **cell** and a size of 1x3.

```
>> whos person

  Name       Size            Bytes  Class    Attributes
  person     1x3               606  cell
```

So then, the question becomes, how do we get the person's name? You could be forgiven for thinking that the name is actually the first element of the array. Indeed if you type **person(1)** you get something that looks very much like a string. However, what you get back is not quite a string, as can be verified by using **whos** again:

```
>> person(1)

ans =
     'John'
```

```
>> whos ans

  Name      Size             Bytes  Class    Attributes
  ans       1x1                120  cell
```

What you got is a cell from the cell array. If you want to get the actual value, instead of using round parentheses, you use curly braces, so writing `person{1}` gives us the name and we can immediately verify that it is, in fact, a string:

```
>> person{1}

ans =
John

>> whos ans

  Name      Size             Bytes  Class    Attributes
  ans       1x4                  8  char
```

Cell arrays are, essentially, a trick to keep different types of data within an array. If you have just a single type of data (say, numeric data), it is best to just use ordinary arrays. We will take a more in-depth look at arrays in Chapter 4.

Function Handles

A function handle is a variable, but instead of storing a numeric or textual value, it actually points to a different function. If you are used to ordinary programming, you can think of a function handle as a function pointer or a delegate. For example, you can define a variable that points to the **sin** function and then use it for invocation.

```
>> s=@sin;
>> s(pi/2)

ans =
     1
```

One thing you can do with function handles is quickly define functions—instead of writing a full declaration (and we will get to function declarations when we discuss scripts), you simply define a handle providing its body (also known as an anonymous function).

```
>> sumOver3 = @(x,y) (x+y)/3

sumOver3 =
```

```
@(x,y)(x+y)/3
```

In the previous definition, the parentheses that follow the **@** sign contain the expected function parameters, and those parameters are subsequently used to perform the calculations. Now I can invoke this function with two parameters:

```
>> sumOver3(2,1)

ans =
       1
```

One reason to use function handles is to pass functions into other functions. This method is often used by MATLAB's "function functions" such as minimization or optimization routines.

Let us make another function that also takes two parameters plus a function, adds 1 to every parameter, then applies the function.

```
>> incApply = @(x,y,f) f(x+1,y+1)

incApply =
     @(x,y,f)f(x+1,y+1)
```

We can now use our **sumOver3** function as a parameter to invoke this new function:

```
>> incApply(2,1,sumOver3)

ans =
           1.66666666666667
```

Chapter 3 Basic Syntax

All the work you do in MATLAB will involve the use of variables, so we will begin by looking at the ways in which variables are declared and manipulated.

Just like any other programming language, MATLAB has different operators for doing different things, so we will take a look at the ones that matter most. Don't worry, there aren't that many of those. Next, we will talk about flow control—things like **if** and **switch** statements and **for** and **while** loops. We will finish the chapter with a discussion of exception handling.

Working with Variables

When working with any kind of computation in MATLAB, we make use of variables. A variable is essentially a storage location: it can store a numeric value, a character, an array, or can refer to a more advanced construct such as a function or structure.

Variables typically have names. A variable name in MATLAB has to start with a letter followed by a zero, more letters, digits, or underscores. Any name is valid except names that have been taken by MATLAB keywords (e.g., **if** or **for**).

There is one variable in MATLAB that you simply cannot avoid meeting: it's called **ans** and it stores the result of the last calculation, assuming that the calculation actually returned a value that was not specifically assigned to another variable. Indeed, it's also possible to assign the **ans** variable, though this is perhaps not the best idea, as it's likely to be overwritten at any moment.

```
>> 2+3

ans =
     5
>> ans*ans

ans =
    25
```

In addition to **ans**, you can specify the name of the variable to assign a value to:

```
>> z = 6 * 7

z =
    42
```

It's also possible to assign multiple variables at once. The function that is responsible for this is called **deal**, and is used to define, on a single line, an assignment of either same or different values to multiple variables. Variables must be declared in square brackets, separated by a comma:

```
>> [x,y] = deal(142)

x =
    142
y =
    142

>> [a,b,c] = deal(1,2,3)

a =
    1
b =
    2
c =
    3
```

Variable Data Import and Export

The state of all the variables in your workspace can be saved into a special kind of file that stores MATLAB Formatted Data. This file has a **.mat** extension, and essentially contains a snapshot of the workspace. To work with these files using the Command Window, you can use the **save** and **load** functions. These can be used without parameters (in which case the file name used is **matlab.mat**), or you can specify your own filename. You can also use **save** and **load** to store individual variables in MAT data files.

In addition to MATLAB Formatted Data, you can also import files in known data formats—not just CSV and the like, but also image data, movies, and many other formats. You can find the Import Data button on the ribbon:

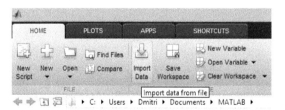

The import process can be customized via the UI (for example, you can tell MATLAB to correctly interpret a particular date/time format), and you can also generate the code that actually performs the import, which is super-useful if you want to share both your script files and data.

Basic Operators

Since MATLAB is a programming language, basic mathematical operations (addition, subtraction, multiplication, and division) use the predictable +, -, * and / operators. Just as in ordinary math, round parentheses can be used to group operations. Square brackets and curly braces are reserved for other uses (numeric and cell arrays, respectively).

```
>> 2*(3+4)

ans =
    14
```

For taking **a** to the power of **b**, MATLAB uses the ^ (hat or circumflex) symbol. MATLAB also has the (somewhat bizarre) back-division operator \ (backslash). This operator has a special meaning for matrices, but for "scalar" values, **a\b** simply means the same as **b/a**. It is probably not a good idea to use this operator for this purpose, unless you deliberately want to obfuscate your code.

Each of the aforementioned operators also has an *elementwise* equivalent prefixed by a dot (e.g., **.+**, **./** and so on). We will discuss elementwise operators later on in the book.

The single = (equals) operator is used for assigning values, e.g. `meaningOfLife = 42`. If you want to compare two values, you use the == operator instead or, if you want to check that the values are different, use ~=, which is the equivalent of the $\neq$ sign. Speaking of comparisons, MATLAB also supports the < and > operators as well as the "or equal" <= and >= counterparts (equivalent to $\leq$ and $\geq$ in math notation). Note that comparisons yield a **0** or a **1** indicating false and true respectively, but the result is not an integer, but a single-byte `logical` value:

```
>> 1 == 2

ans =
    0
>> whos ans

  Name      Size            Bytes  Class      Attributes
  ans       1x1                 1  logical
```

Values of `logical` type can be treated as numeric values for the purposes of calculations, but any numeric operation on them will yield a **double** value.

It's also important to note that you can supply numeric values to constructs that expect logical values (e.g., **if** statements). In this case, MATLAB treats the value of 0 to mean **false** and any other value to mean **true**. I wouldn't recommend using this feature, though, as it can lead to difficult-to-spot errors.

Now let's talk about the **,** (comma) and **;** (semicolon) operators. MATLAB, unlike many programming languages, does not require you to terminate your statements with the semicolon. However, if you do not, the resulting value of a calculation will be printed to the command window. If you do terminate the statement with a semicolon, though, nothing gets printed to the command window:

```
>> x=1

x =
    1

>> y=2;
```

The comma operator is used to separate parameters to a function, but it also has a more obscure use case—when you want to separate several statements on a single line, but you **do** want command window output. In this case, simply separate the statements with a comma instead:

```
>> x=1, y=2

x =
    1
y =
    2
```

The **%** (percent) operator is used to create comments, and is particularly useful in scripts. Everything following the **%** sign on a particular line is ignored by MATLAB for purposes of execution, but the operator does have special uses when it comes to publishing scripts (discussed later).

Finally there is the **!** (exclamation point) operator. This operator is used to issue commands to the operating system and, as you can imagine, its function depends on the OS you're running. For example, on Windows, we can issue a command that lists the contents of the current directory:

```
>> !dir

 Volume in drive C has no label.
 Volume Serial Number is 40A1-C189

 Directory of C:\Users\Dmitri\Documents\MATLAB
```

```
23/01/2014  22:46   <DIR>          .
23/01/2014  22:46   <DIR>          ..
14/09/2013  15:53   <DIR>          html
11/10/2013  11:25            199 Untitled.m
               1 File(s)          199 bytes
               3 Dir(s)  193,780,895,744 bytes free
```

 Note: MATLAB actually has its own dir **function, so you can call it without the exclamation mark and get a similar (but not identical) result.**

Flow Control

Let us begin with the if statement—this statement lets you check a condition (e.g., the result of a comparison) and perform an operation depending on whether the result is true or false (remember that in MATLAB these are denoted by 1 and 0 respectively). For example, if we have a temperature reading and we need to determine whether or not it's hot outside, we can write the following check:

```
t = getTemperatureValue();

if t > 100
   disp('hot')
end
```

This piece of code checks the value of **t**, and if it is greater than 100, outputs the line 'hot' to the command window. We can add additional checks to the if statement, checking for example if it is cold. To do this, we add an **elseif** clause:

```
if t > 100
   disp('hot')
elseif t < 0
   disp('cold')
end
```

Now, if the first check fails, the second check is performed. If neither are successful, though (for example, **t=50**), nothing happens. Now, if we want to execute some other piece of code if none of the conditions in our if statement are true, we can add an **else** clause:

```
if t > 100
   disp('hot')
elseif t < 0
   disp('cold')
else
```

```
   disp('ok')
end
```

A temperature measurement is a continuous value, but if we want to investigate a discrete set of values—say, a country's dialing codes—we might want to use another kind of control flow structure called a **switch** statement. This statement tries to match a variable's content against a set of discrete values. For example, to determine the country name from the country code we can write:

```
switch cc
  case 44
    disp('uk')
  case 46
    disp('sweden')
  otherwise
    disp('unknown')
end
```

If the country code is **44**, we print **uk**, if it is 46 we print **sweden**, but if it is equal to some other value that we failed to match against, we print **unknown**. Note that there is no need to explicitly terminate a case in a **switch** statement.

Quite often, we want to cycle through a set of values, performing an operation on each. For example, let us try iteratively adding up numbers from 1 to 500 (not the best way of doing things, but good enough for a demonstration). To cycle through the values, we use a **for** loop:

```
sum = 0;

for i = 1:500
  sum = sum + i;
end

disp(sum)
```

In this example, the variable i takes on all values in the 1 to 500 range, and at each iteration, this value is added to **sum**.

A **while** loop is similar to the **for** loop, with the difference that instead of iterating a set of values, it checks a condition and keeps executing while the condition holds. For example, the following code generates and outputs random values between 0 and 1 while they are less than 0.7:

```
v = rand();

while v < 0.7
  disp(v)
  v = rand();
end
```

As soon as a value greater than or equal to 0.7 is generated, the v < 0.7 check fails and we exit the **while** loop.

Sometimes you might be somewhere in the middle of the loop and want to cut the execution short. In this case, you can execute a **break** statement, which will take you out of the loop and continue executing just after the **end** statement:

```
while 1
  x = rand();
  y = rand();
  if (x + y) > 1.0
    break
  else
    disp([num2str(x) num2str(y)])
  end
end
```

The above rule is deliberately made to run forever by providing a **1** (true) in the condition, but we break out of a loop as soon as the sum of two random values exceeds **1.0**. Similarly, had we wanted to avoid printing the **x** and **y** values inside this loop, we could replace the **break** keyword with **continue**, which would simply take us to the start of the loop.

Exception Handling

Anytime you do something MATLAB doesn't like, you end up with an exception. An exception is an indication that something went wrong and MATLAB doesn't know how to deal with it. For example, a division by zero is not an exception, since MATLAB can just give you the **inf** constant, but if you try to read a variable that doesn't exist, there's no way to gracefully handle this, so MATLAB just fails with an error message.

```
>> disp(abc); disp('done')

Undefined function or variable 'abc'.
```

After an exception is generated, all other statements that follow it will not execute. To avoid this situation, I can actually try to catch this exception if I think that it might happen. The way to do it is to place the code where exceptions can occur in a try-catch block:

```
try
  disp(abc);
catch e
  disp (['oops! ' e.message])
end

disp('done')
```

If I execute this, assuming that the variable **abc** does not exist, I get the following output:

```
oops! Undefined function or variable 'abc'.
done
```

It's worth explaining what's going on above. When we catch the exception, it gets stored in a variable (in our case, it's called **e**). The exception is itself a class object (we discuss classes in Chapter 7) with detailed information about the error:

```
e =
  MException with properties:

    identifier: 'MATLAB:UndefinedFunction'
       message: 'Undefined function or variable 'abc'.'
         cause: {}
         stack: [1x1 struct]
```

As you can see, the exception has a type **MException**, and it has several fields, including an identifier, the actual message (that's what we printed to the command window) as well as the **stack** (which happens to be an array of **structs**), which tells you who threw the exception and where:

```
>> e.stack

ans =
    file: 'C:\Users\Dmitri\Documents\MATLAB\Untitled.m'
    name: 'Untitled'
    line: 2
```

It's also possible to **rethrow** exceptions and, needless to say, you can create and throw exceptions of your own using the **error** function.

Chapter 4 Arrays and Matrices

We have now come to arguably the most important chapter in the book. Remember, MATLAB stands for MATrix LABoratory, so work with matrices is central to just about everything that goes on in MATLAB. In this chapter, we get to look at the way matrices are created and manipulated, and some common operations that apply to them.

Terminology

Before we get started, remember that all variables in MATLAB are, in fact, arrays. What I mean is that when you write x=5, you may as well have written x=[5], and both of these effectively imply a 1×1 array.

In our discussions, we'll use the terms *array* and *matrix* interchangeably. We will, however, use the term *vector* to mean a one-dimensional array. In this case we'll also use the term *row vector* to mean a horizontal array that takes up one row:

$$[1 \quad 2 \quad 3]$$

and the term *column vector* to mean an array that takes up one column:

$$\begin{bmatrix} 4 \\ 5 \\ 6 \end{bmatrix}$$

One-Dimensional Arrays

The simplest way to initialize an array is to declare a variable and initialize it using square brackets, separating the elements with spaces and/or commas:

```
>> x = [1, 2 3 4]

x =
     1     2     3     4
```

What we've got is a row vector of 4 elements. If we want a column vector instead, we write roughly the same thing, but instead of spaces we separate the entries with semicolons:

```
>> y = [1;2;3;4]
```

```
y =
    1
    2
    3
    4
```

An entirely different way of initializing arrays is to use the colon operator. This operator lets you define arrays containing sequences of values. For example:

```
>> z = 1:10

z =
    1    2    3    4    5    6    7    8    9    10
```

The above has created a row vector with elements 1 to 10. Curiously enough, this approach also works with strings, so you can, for example, declare an array going from **a** to **z**, which will yield... you guessed it, a string with all the characters from a to z!

```
>> 'a':'z'

ans =
abcdefghijklmnopqrstuvwxyz
```

Using the column operator, you can specify not only the start and end of the range of values, but also the step size. For example, here we generate all odd numbers from 1 to 15:

```
>> 1:2:15

ans =
    1    3    5    7    9    11    13    15
```

Note that if you want a decreasing set of values, the step size needs to be negative, so if you want the above numbers in descending order, you need to write **15:-2:1**.

```
>> 15:-2:1

ans =
    15    13    11    9    7    5    3    1
```

And that's not all. There is another command for creating a set of values in a specific range. The function **linspace** subdivides a range into several points (100 by default). The third parameter to the function lets you define how many points you want:

```
>> linspace(0,1,11)
```

```
ans =
  Columns 1 through 8
        0    0.1000    0.2000    0.3000    0.4000    0.5000    0.6000    0.7000
  Columns 9 through 11
    0.8000    0.9000    1.0000
```

In this call, we've generated 11 equally spaced points on a [0; 1] range.

💡 *Tip: When using Linspace, you typically want to have the number of points to be one more than the number of parts you want to divide the range into. For example, if you want to split a range into 100 parts, consider specifying 101 points.*

Two-Dimensional Arrays

Now let's move on to two-dimensional arrays. Such an array can be initialized with a combination of spaces. For example, to create the matrix $\begin{bmatrix} 1 & 2 \\ 3 & 4 \end{bmatrix}$ we write:

```
>> g = [1 2;3 4]

g =
     1     2
     3     4
```

Having made a matrix, we can use the **size** function to take a measurement of its dimensions:

```
>> size(g)

ans =
     2     2
```

Once again, MATLAB has special functions for creating two-dimensional arrays. First of these is the **zeros** function, which creates a zero-initialized matrix:

```
>> zeros(3,2)

ans =
     0     0
     0     0
```

```
     0      0
```

Note that, when specifying dimensions, you first specify the number of rows (3) and then the number of columns (2). Had you specified only a single argument, that argument would be taken for *both* dimensions – in other words, `zeros(3)` creates a 3x3 array. The function `zeros` also has its counterpart called **ones**. I leave it to the reader to figure out what kind of matrix it creates. And, similarly to these, the functions `inf`, `nan`, and `rand`, when provided size arguments, create matrices correspondingly filled with infinity, NaN, and random values.

Jumping ahead a little bit, it is important to realize that functions such as `zeros` can create arrays of any dimensions. We have made a 2D array above, but we could easily create a 3D array by providing an array of dimensions as an array as the first and only argument to the function:

```
>> zeros(2,3,2)

ans(:,:,1) =
      0      0      0
      0      0      0
ans(:,:,2) =
      0      0      0
      0      0      0
```

This code effectively creates a 2×3×2 array. Don't worry; we will get to multi-dimensional arrays very soon.

Meanwhile, here is another special array-building function called **eye**, which creates an identity matrix:

```
>> eye(3)

ans =
      1      0      0
      0      1      0
      0      0      1
```

Invoked with a single argument, it has created a square 3×3 array for us. Had we specified two arguments, it would have created a rectangular array that would have zeroes in all places except the diagonal.

Addressing, Manipulation, and Slicing

Now that we know how to create arrays, let us discuss ways of manipulating them. Let us make an array from 1 to 100. (Note that we have terminated the statement with a semicolon here to suppress the output. Had we not done this, we would get 100 numbers in the command window.)

```
>> x=1:100;
```

To get a single element of the array, you just write the name of the array followed by an index of the element. For example, to get the first element of the array **x** we write:

```
>> x(1)

ans =
    1
```

📝 *Note: Array indices in MATLAB start with 1, not with a 0.*

To get all elements from position 5 to position 10, we can simply write:

```
>> x(5:10)

ans =
    5    6    7    8    9    10
```

What we end up with is a brand new array of six elements corresponding to positions 5 to 10 in the original array.

There is also a special variable end that you can use to indicate the last element of the array. For example, to get the last ten elements of the array, we can write:

```
>> x(end-9:end)

ans =
    91   92   93   94   95   96   97   98   99   100
```

It's also possible to filter elements of an array by specifying a precondition. For example, here's a way of taking all odd values from 1 to 10:

```
>> x = 1:10

x =
    1    2    3    4    5    6    7    8    9    10

>> y = x(mod(x,2) == 1)

y =
    1    3    5    7    9
```

There are quite a few things happening in this example. First of all, it's worth noting that mod is a *vectorized* function, meaning that for each of the elements in the input array it will generate as many in the output. The operator == is also perfectly happy to work in a vectorized manner, being applied to each element of mod's output in turn. Finally, since the end result of a comparison is a logical value, this illustrates another way of indexing into an array: by providing a set of true/false values as indices, we filter the array, leaving only those elements for which the corresponding parameter value is **true**.

As you may have guessed, not only can we access elements of the array, we can modify them too. Changing a single element is easy—you just write x(10)=123 and that's your 10th element changed. But, interestingly enough, we can also change a subset of an array by providing a new array (obviously, the sizes must match). For example, to reverse the order of the first five elements of our array, we can write

```
>> x(1:5)=5:-1:1

x =
  Columns 1 through 14
    5    4    3    2    1    6    7    8    9    10    11    12    13
14
    (other columns omitted)
```

This operation essentially creates a range of values from 5 to 1 with a step of -1 and then places those values in positions 1 through 5 of the original array.

Manipulation of 2D arrays follows very similar ideas. Consider the following array:

```
>> x = [1 2;3 4]

x =
    1    2
    3    4
```

I can index its elements using either two indices (corresponding to its row and column) or I can use just a single index, in which case the array is traversed in column order (meaning we first traverse the first column top-to-bottom, then the second, and so on):

```
>> x(2,1)

ans =
    3

>> x(3)

ans =
    2

>> x(1:end)

ans =
    1    3    2    4
```

You can also get the whole row or the whole column of a 2D (or indeed N-d, where N>1) array by simply replacing the specifier for the other dimensions with a : (colon) operator, which is the operator that's used to indicate a "don't care" or "give me everything" value. For example, to get the first row, we write:

```
>> x(1,:)

ans =
    1    2
```

This invocation essentially says "give me something from row 1, and all columns." And that's exactly what you get. Needless to say, modifications to 2D arrays happen in just the same way as for 1D arrays, so to replace the first column with the values [5, 6] you can write:

```
>> x(:,1) = [5;6]

x =
    5    2
    6    4
```

When it comes to removing elements from the array, one possibility is to set the elements you want to remove to [], which is an empty array:

```
x =
    1    2    3    4

>> x(3) = []

x =
    1    2    4
```

It's also possible to take the diagonal of a matrix with the **diag** function. Here is a rather convoluted way of creating a column vector filled with 1s:

```
>> diag(eye(3))

ans =
    1
    1
    1
```

The **diag** function simplifies work with diagonal matrices and actually works both ways: not only can you take the diagonal of an existing matrix, you can turn a vector with a matrix containing zeros in all elements except the diagonal:

```
>> diag([1 2 3])

ans =
    1    0    0
    0    2    0
    0    0    3
```

Sorting and Reshaping

To illustrate the idea of sorting the elements in the array, I will make a 5×5 magic square using MATLAB's **magic** function:

```
>> z = magic(5)

z =
    17    24     1     8    15
    23     5     7    14    16
     4     6    13    20    22
    10    12    19    21     3
    11    18    25     2     9
```

Just in case you're wondering, a magic square has a property in which all its rows and columns have elements that add up to the same number. We aren't going to exploit this property for our demonstrations, though—instead, let's try sorting the array. To sort each of the columns in the array, we can simply use **z** as an argument to the **sort** function:

```
>> sort(z)

ans =
```

```
     4      5      1      2      3
    10      6      7      8      9
    11     12     13     14     15
    17     18     19     20     16
    23     24     25     21     22
```

Now each of the columns appears in order. If we wanted to sort each of the rows, however, we would need to explicitly specify the dimension to sort on in our call to **sort**: the second parameter value of 1 means rows, 2 – columns.

```
>> sort(z,2)

ans =
     1      8     15     17     24
     5      7     14     16     23
     4      6     13     20     22
     3     10     12     19     21
     2      9     11     18     25
```

And this gives us a matrix where each row's values appear in ascending order.

Now, let's say we've got two simple arrays:

```
>> x = [1 2];
>> y = [3 4];
```

We can merge these two arrays into a single array. To concatenate these two arrays together, we simply make a new array with **x** and **y** being featured as its elements:

```
>> [x y]

ans =
     1      2      3      4

>> [x;y]

ans =
     1      2
     3      4

>> [x y;y x]

ans =
     1      2      3      4
```

```
   3      4      1      2
```

Note that, in the last example, I have included the original arrays in the new array more than once. This is perfectly legal, and simply causes repetition of the contents of the source arrays.

Now, suppose you want enlarge an array. How would you do it? Well, the simplest way is to assign an element of the matrix that doesn't yet exist—this immediately reshapes the array to accommodate the new value:

```
>> whos x

  Name        Size            Bytes  Class      Attributes
  x           1x2                16  double

>> x(3,3) = 12

x =
     1     2     0
     0     0     0
     0     0    12

>> whos x

  Name        Size            Bytes  Class      Attributes
  x           3x3                72  double
```

As you can see from the output, a 1×2 array was magically resized into a 3×3 array when a new element was added.

If you need to shrink the array, simply take a slice of it! For example, to get back to the original array, all I need to do is take the first two column elements of the first row:

```
>> x(1,1:2)

ans =
     1     2
```

MATLAB also has a set of very specific matrix operations, such as the ability to rotate a matrix 90 degrees:

```
>> z = eye(3);
>> rot90(z)

ans =
     0     0     1
     0     1     0
```

```
       1     0     0
```

Last, but certainly not least, MATLAB has a **reshape** function. This function takes an array as if it were one-dimensional by iterating its dimensions, and then reshaping the array into as many dimensions as you specify. Naturally, the number of elements in the original and requested arrays must match:

```
>> x = magic(4);
>> reshape(x,2,8)

ans =
    16     9     2     7     3     6    13    12
     5     4    11    14    10    15     8     1
```

This piece of code, for example, takes a 4×4 magic square and reshapes it into a 2×8 array. Likewise, we could easily reshape the square into, e.g., a 1×16 array or a 2×4×2 array.

As with the **reshape** function, it's also possible to turn a matrix into a column vector by addressing its elements with a single colon:

```
>> x = magic(2)
x =
     1     3
     4     2
>> x(:)
ans =
     1
     4
     3
     2
```

Of course, this shouldn't be particularly surprising: we already mentioned that multi-dimensional arrays can be indexed with a single value, so the result of getting all the values should not be unexpected.

Transposition and Inversion

Transposition is a very common matrix operation. Essentially, it reflects the matrix along the diagonal, so each element swaps its row and column positions. Strictly speaking, MATLAB has a **transpose** function defined for this purpose, but it is much easier to use a single dash (') for the exact same purpose (assuming non-complex data):

```
>> x = [1 2;3 4]

x =
     1     2
     3     4

>> x'

ans =
     1     3
     2     4
```

Transposition is also useful for defining column vectors, since the **x:y** notation gives you a row vector by default:

```
>> (1:5)'

ans =
     1
     2
     3
     4
     5
```

Note the use of round brackets above—the ' operator has higher precedence than :, so you cannot write **1:5'** because it effectively means **1:5'**.

Another common operation is matrix inversion, which, given a matrix X gives you a matrix Y satisfying the relation $YX = I$ (where I is the identity matrix, **eye**). The inverse matrix is found by either using the **inv** function or taking the original matrix to the power of -1:

```
>> x = [-1 1;0 1];
>> x^-1

ans =
    -1     1
     0     1

>> ans*x

ans =
     1     0
     0     1
```

Elementwise Operators

Elementwise operators are central to working with matrices in MATLAB. The best way to illustrate what they are for is with an example. Let us make two 2×2 matrices:

```
>> x=[1 2;3 4];
>> y=[5 6;7 8];
```

Now, the expression **x*y** implies multiplication of the two matrices according to linear algebra matrix multiplication rules (matrix dimensions should, of course, agree), but what if you just want each of the elements in **x** to be multiplied by the corresponding element in **y** (also known as a Hadamard product)? This is what elementwise operators are for. Essentially, all we have to do is put a period (.) in front of the multiplication operator, and here is what we get:

```
>> x.*y

ans =
     5    12
    21    32
```

Elementwise operators are critical when working with any sort of data sets, and warrant additional examples. For instance, let's say we put $100 into a bank account with a 5 percent interest rate paid annually. Now we want to know how much money we'll have after 1..10 years. Our first temptation is to write something like:

```
>> 100*(1+0.05)^(1:10)

Error using  ^
Inputs must be a scalar and a square matrix.
To compute elementwise POWER, use POWER (.^) instead.
```

But as you can see, we cannot take a scalar value to the power of an array—this operation simply doesn't make any sense! What we need to do is replace the power operator with its elementwise version so that our scalar value gets raised to each of the powers in turn:

```
>> 100*(1+0.05).^(1:10)

ans =
  Columns 1 through 5
       105.00        110.25        115.76        121.55        127.63
  Columns 6 through 10
       134.01        140.71        147.75        155.13        162.89
```

That's much better.

Solving Linear Systems of Equations

One of the common uses of matrices is to use them to solve linear systems of equations. For example, consider this set of equations:

$$x + y = 10$$
$$x - y = 4$$

We can use matrices to represent this equation in the form of $AX = B$ where A is the matrix of multipliers and B is the matrix of results:

MATLAB offers us the option to solve this system using the `linsolve` function. All we need to do is feed in the coefficients:

```
>> a = [1,1; 1,-1]

a =
      1      1
      1     -1
>> b

b =
     10
      4
>> linsolve(a,b)

ans =
      7
      3
```

And now we're going to meet another operator! We've already seen it as the back-division operator, but the array-specific \ (backslash) operator that also solves the equation $AX = B$ can be more efficient by using Gaussian elimination without producing an inverse of the matrix. Thus, it's faster than calculating `inv(a)*b`:

```
>> a\b

ans =
      7
      3
```

Sparse Matrices

In addition to ordinary matrices, MATLAB also supports sparse matrices. These are typically large matrices that have only a small percentage of non-zero entries. Sparse matrices are defined by providing the **sparse** function three arrays containing the coordinates of the element (one array for **i**, another for **j**) and the element values themselves:

```
>> i = [2,4,6];
>> j = [1,3,5];
>> v = [-1 200 33.7];
>> sparse(i,j,v)

ans =
   (2,1)      -1.0000
   (4,3)     200.0000
   (6,5)      33.7000
```

A sparse matrix can also be turned into a proper, fully-specified matrix using the **full** function:

```
>> full(ans)

ans =

        0        0        0        0        0
  -1.0000        0        0        0        0
        0        0        0        0        0
        0        0 200.0000        0        0
        0        0        0        0        0
        0        0        0        0  33.7000
```

One useful command for generally figuring out what is happening in an array is **spy**. This command lets you visualize the elements in an array on a graph, and is particularly useful for viewing sparse matrices. For example, spying on a 4×4 identity matrix gives us the following diagram:

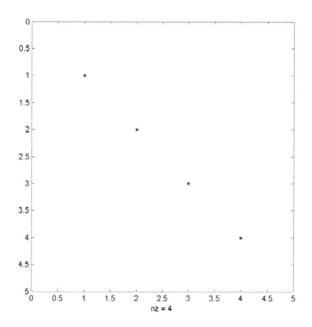

Figure 10: Using the spy command on a 4×4 identity matrix.

As you may have guessed, dots represent non-zero elements while zeros do not get any dots. Note also the **x** and **y** coordinates, which correspond to matrix element positions. Oh, and make sure you don't forget the arguments—if you just type **spy**, you're in for a surprise.

Higher Dimensions

As you may have guessed, arrays of dimensions higher than two cannot be efficiently represented on a two-dimensional computer monitor, but this doesn't mean that we can't work with them.

The simplest way to make a 3D array is to use one of the functions that takes array dimension parameters. For example, I can use the **reshape** function to create an array of eight values and shape them into a 2×2×2 array:

```
>> reshape(1:8, [2 2 2])
```

```
ans(:,:,1) =
          1.00          3.00
          2.00          4.00
ans(:,:,2) =
          5.00          7.00
          6.00          8.00
```

Note the visual representation: since a 3D array cannot be efficiently represented in 2D space, we get to see each of its 2D slices in turn.

Other MATLAB functions such as **ones**, **zeros**, and various random number generators also allow you to specify the dimensions of the matrix that's being generated.

Another way of creating a matrix with more than two dimensions is to simply add an extra dimension to an existing 2D matrix. For example, you can start out with a 2×2 matrix:

```
>> x = [1 2;3 4]

x =
          1.00          2.00
          3.00          4.00
```

And now, you can simply "splice" another 2×2 matrix into x's third dimension:

```
>> x(:,:,2) = [4 5;6 7]

x(:,:,1) =
          1.00          2.00
          3.00          4.00
x(:,:,2) =
          4.00          5.00
          6.00          7.00
```

As you can imagine, the approaches outlined here work for higher dimensions as well.

Chapter 5 Working with Scripts

There are two ways of interacting with MATLAB. One is to simply type things into the Command Window—that way, you get to see the results immediately, but it becomes difficult (though not impossible) to write complicated programs. An alternative is to use **scripts**—separate files that make up your program. MATLAB scripts typically have the **.m** extension, and are plain-text files that MATLAB lets you edit, execute, and debug.

Script Templates

The simplest way to create a script in MATLAB is to click the **New Script** button (or the Ctrl+N shortcut). However, MATLAB also gives us a few script templates—ready-made script files representing certain constructs that we might want to create:

Figure 11: New object drop-down list.

It's really only the top few options that we are interested in. In addition to creating a script, you can also create a **Function**, in which case you'll simply get a stub for a function definition; you can make an **Example**, which is just a script file with nicely formatted documentation, ready for publication; next up is a **Class**, which is an OOP construct (see Chapter 7).

Other elements in this menu come from various toolboxes and aren't necessarily script files.

So let's use the Function template to create a reusable function for solving a quadratic equation:

```
function [x1,x2] = SolveQuadratic(a,b,c)
%SolveQuadratic Solves a quadratic equation
  disc = b*b - 4*a*c;
  x1 = (-b+sqrt(disc))/(2*a);
  x2 = (-b-sqrt(disc))/(2*a);
end
```

Let's examine this function definition. First of all, immediately after the function keyword, we list all the values that the function is going to return, within square brackets (brackets are unnecessary if there's only a single return value). In this case, these are the x1 and x2 values, which are solutions to the quadratic equation.

Then, after the = sign, we have the name of the function. Note that the file name should ideally match the function name, so the **SolveQuadratic** function should be saved in a script file called **SolveQuadratic.m**. The name of the function is followed by a set of function arguments in parentheses, separated by commas. When calling this function, the caller has to provide exactly as many arguments as are specified here (i.e. three).

The comment line right after the function declaration essentially provides documentation for whoever will be using this function. This is called the "H1 Line" in MATLAB. When we open the Function Browser for this function, what we'll get is documentation generated from these comments:

Figure 12: Documentation for our SolveQuadratic function.

Now, after saving the **.m** file, we can start using the function, assuming that the file is available on MATLAB's path:

```
>> SolveQuadratic(1,10,16)

ans =
    -2
```

Oops! That's not quite right, is it? We were expecting two solutions but got just one (which happens in some quadratic equations, but still, we were expecting two values). The problem is that we invoked a function that returns two values, but didn't specify storage for them, so MATLAB just took the first value and saved it in **ans**. Not very nice, is it? Well, the correct way to get both of the values is to assign them to variables like so:

```
>> [x,y] = SolveQuadratic(1,10,16)

x =
    -2

y =
    -8
```

That's much better! This code line effectively declares both x and y on a single line, and, after the function call, both of the variables are ready to be used.

Sections

Before we start running scripts, we need to talk about script sections. These are important and serve two purposes:

- Sections separate your script into several intelligible parts, making it nicer to read. In this regard, you can consider scripts as chapter or section headings of a book.
- You can execute each section separately. This is great for testing out small parts of a large script.

A section is typically prefixed by **%%** (two percentage signs). As you prefix a section, you'll notice that all the code until the next section is highlighted—this helps you figure out where the section ends.

To execute a section, you can press the **Run Section** button (or Ctrl+Enter). The section that gets executed is the one your cursor is currently in.

Running and Debugging

Running a script is simple—press the **Run** button (or F5), or use the Run Section option to just run part of the script. Of course, you can also run the script from the Command window, so assuming your file **SolveQuadratic.m** is on MATLAB's path, you can just type **SolveQuadratic**, press **Enter**, and your script gets to execute.

While we assume most of our readers to be careful and proficient MATLAB users, errors sometimes do occur and it's often worth checking up on the execution of the program. The first thing worth trying is Debugging—this is the process of being able to stop the program mid-stream and inspect the values of the variables.

Debugging is done using breakpoints—markers that indicate the location where execution should pause. The Breakpoints section on the Editor tab has several options related to breakpoints:

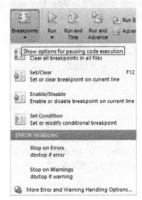

Figure 13: Breakpoint options.

Of most benefit is the Set/Clear option. This creates a breakpoint at the current line in your program. You can also set a breakpoint by pressing F12 or clicking on the margin on the left-hand side of the editor.

```
Editor - C:\Users\Dmitri\Documents\M

 Untitled.m     ×

1 -      x = -2:0.01:2;
2 ● ⇨    y = sqrt(cos(x));
3 -      z = 2;
```

Figure 14: A triggered breakpoint.

One a breakpoint triggers, execution will stop and a green line will indicate the line at which the script was paused. You can then run the program line-by-line or continue execution. Variables can be expected either in the Workspace Window or, as shown above, by simply hovering the mouse over the symbol in the editor.

Profiling

We all get this moment when our program runs slowly for some unknown reason and we want to know why.

If your goal is to simply get a time measurement for a chunk of code, consider using the `tic` and `toc` functions, which start and stop a simple timer:

```
tic
% your code here
toc
```

As soon as you call `toc`, the timer stops and the elapsed time gets printed to the command window:

```
Elapsed time is 1.127136 seconds.
```

> **Note: Since `tic` and `toc` only start/stop measuring time when they are actually invoked, make sure that if you use the Command Window you call them both (and the code to profile in between) in a single statement. Otherwise, you'll be measuring not just your own algorithm, but your typing speed, too!**

If you're after a more complete, comprehensive report on the performance of your script, you need to profile your script. MATLAB has a built-in profiler that you can use to determine which part of your script took the most time—this lets you fine-tune the bottlenecks in your scripts and thus improve their overall performance. You can start profiling with the Run and Time button—when you press it and execute your script, MATLAB will pop up an additional window containing some metrics of your script's performance:

Profile Summary
Generated 31-Jan-2014 21:52:54 using cpu time.

Function Name	Calls	Total Time	Self Time*	Total Time Plot (dark band = self time)
Spiral	1	0.144 s	0.003 s	
newplot	1	0.139 s	0.074 s	
newplot>ObserveAxesNextPlot	1	0.065 s	0.002 s	
graphics\private\clo	1	0.063 s	0.007 s	
cla	1	0.063 s	0.000 s	
setdiff	2	0.053 s	0.012 s	

Figure 15: Profile summary.

The profiling summary shown in Figure 15 gives an indication of the number of times a function was invoked and how much time it took together with all the things it called, as well as the amount of time that the function itself spent doing something. It is possible to click each of the functions to get detailed information about the particular lines and how much time they took.

Of course, you can also invoke the profiler from the Command Window:

```
>> profile on
>> myscript
>> profile off
>> profile viewer
```

Publishing

Imagine you are working on a complicated algorithm and your manager suddenly wants a status update on your work. With MATLAB's Publishing feature, what you can do is click a single button, and your script, together with all the plots and calculations it made, gets packaged as a document ready to be sent off.

It is possible to publish MATLAB scripts into various types of documents, including HTML, LaTeX, PDF, and others. If you want to publish your script to a document, click the **Publish** tab, choose **Publish**, **Settings** and choose the format and other options you need:

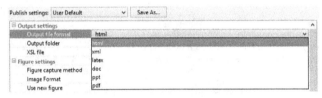

Figure 1: Script file publishing formats.

Now, regardless of the output format you choose, it's important to realize what actually happens with your code as it gets published. Here are the key processes that take place:

- All section headings become top-level headings **with the exception of the first one**. The first section you create becomes the title heading of the whole document.
- Comments immediately after the section heading turn into paragraphs of text. Note that MATLAB supports additional formatting in such comments, such as options for making text bold or italic, making hyperlinks, or even including LaTeX formulae.
- Any executable code that you have gets placed into the document. MATLAB applies some syntax highlighting so the code looks nice.
- All code you wrote gets executed. Output error/warning messages also end up in the published output.
- Any images you generate also get included in the document.

To generate a document, simply press **Publish**—it really is that simple.

A note on LaTeX

To render nice formulae need to use LaTeX but, unfortunately, MATLAB gives you no help with th syntax. Your options are follows:

1. Use the `latex` functic from the Symbolic Toolt

2. Create formulae in m (a separate environmen exists as a companion t MATLAB) and export frc there.

3. Use a proper LaTeX editor such as LyX.

Comparison and Search

The ability to search for a particular file is built into all operating systems, but MATLAB also has its own facilities for searching either for a particular file name or for files containing specific text. The Home ribbon tab has a Find Files button that lets you do exactly this:

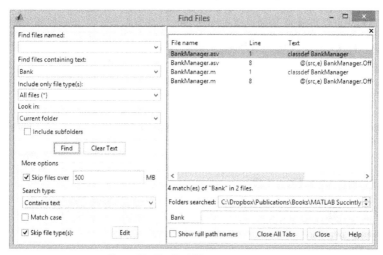

Figure 17: The Find Files window.

Just below that button is the Compare button, which lets you compare two files—handy for seeing changes as you update your code:

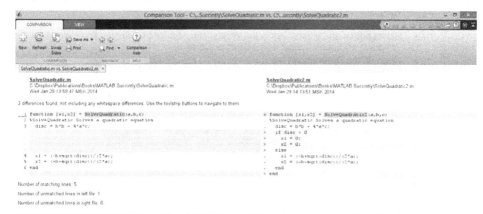

Figure 18: The File Comparison window. Added lines are shown in green, changed lines in red.

Chapter 6 Data Visualization

The simplest way to plot some data is to do it via the UI, so we will begin this chapter by learning how to prepare data for plotting and then using the ribbon interface to quickly plot the data. We will then move to doing plots entirely from the console and discuss all the different ways that one can plot data. We will also discuss the idea of plotting symbolic functions, even though this is part of the Symbolic Toolbox.

We will then discuss figure windows and the ways one can have several sets of data plotted on a single graph. Then we will look at adding various text annotations such as labels to the plots, as well as ways of combining multiple plots in a single window. I will then show some of MATLAB's functionality for editing the plot in the figure window.

To finish it all off, we will discuss one potential problem with MATLAB: the fact that it doesn't automatically generate origin axes lines.

Plotting via the UI

Before we're able to plot anything in MATLAB, we need to define the data that we are going to plot. Let's do a 2D plot of the function $y = x$^3. The typical way of doing this is to define a range of x values, then calculate a range of y values, then plot the two:

```
>> x = linspace(-10,10,101);
>> y = x .^ 3;
```

Having calculated the coordinate values, we can now do the following:

- Select both **x** and **y** variables in the Workspace window (to select multiple variables, on Windows, you need to hold either **Shift** or **Control**).
- Open up the **Plots** ribbon tab.
- Click one of the ready-made plot types, in our case the one called **plot**:

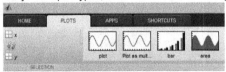

Figure 19: Various plot options.

Here's what we get:

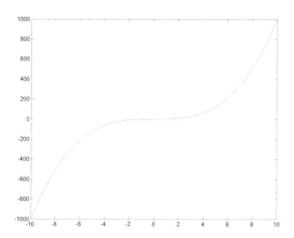

Figure 20: A plot of the function $f(x) = x$^3.

The set of buttons you can press on the Plots tab corresponds to the data you have selected. For example, you cannot do a 3D plot from two sets of arrays. Instead, to do a 3D plot, we need to define something called a mesh grid. The correspondingly named `meshgrid` command creates two 2D arrays, each of which is a grid of values in a range we define. For example:

```
>> [x,y] = meshgrid(-10:0.5:10,-10:0.5:10)
```

Note that the function returns not one but two values—the previous code illustrates how two values are stored in corresponding variables. So what we have now is variables **x** and **y**, each of which is a 41×41 array. In the array **x**, each row has values going from -10 to 10 (all rows are identical), whereas the array **y** has all columns going from -10 to 10.

The reason we're performing this strange manipulation is that we want to do a surface plot, i.e. to calculate the z values from these x and y values. We can now calculate the value of z using elementwise operations:

```
>> z = sin(x) .* sinh(y);
```

And now I can simply select the variable **z** in the workspace and choose the **surf** type of plot to get this:

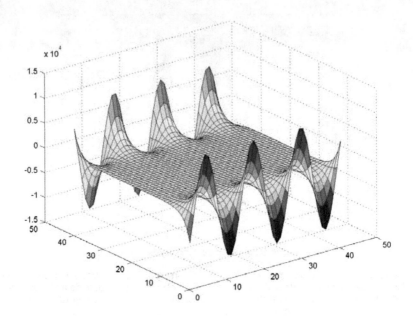

Figure 21: Surface plot of the function $f(x, y) = \sin x \; \sinh y$.

Note once again that, as you selected the z value, the range of possible plots in the Plots ribbon tab was correspondingly adjusted. Oh, just for fun, try **surf(membrane)**... does the image look familiar? (Hint: try **logo**, too.)

Simple Two-Dimensional Plots

If you look at the Command Window as you press those plot buttons, you'll see that all they do is send MATLAB certain plot commands such as **plot** or **surf**. We are now going to stop using the Plots tab altogether and only use the command window, entering the commands by hand.

Most of the 2D plots are done using the **plot** command. For example, say we want to plot $y = \sin x$ using a solid red line. You can simply type the following into the Command Window:

```
>> x = linspace(-10, 10, 101);
>> y = sin(x);
```

```
>> plot(x, y, '-r')
```

The '-r' above plots a red line. I'll explain the syntax in a moment; let's continue plotting things for now.

Now, the **plot** command continues to recycle the same window, so if we did another plot, it would overwrite the old one. How to show both **sin** and **cos** on the same figure window? For that, we need to use the **hold** command. **hold on** causes all plots to go to the same window, and **hold off** correspondingly reverts this behavior. So let's plot $y = \cos x$ in blue over our existing plot:

```
>> hold on
>> y2 = cos(x);
>> plot(x,y2,'-b')
```

Here is the end result:

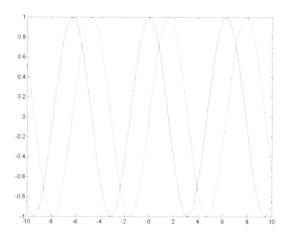

Figure 22: The functions $f(x) = \sin x$ and $\cos x$ rendered in red and blue respectively.

The last parameter used in both of the **plot** functions above ('-r' and '-b') is a set of options for controlling how the lines are rendered. The dash (-) indicates we need a solid line (there are also dotted : and dashed -- styles available), and 'r' and 'b' refer to the red and blue colors respectively (other available colors are g(reen), m(agenta), c(yan), y(ellow) and (blac)k). This is also the location where it's possible to control the shape of the marker for each data point: there are many options such as 'x' (draws a cross) or 'o' (draws a circle) – consult the documentation for more!

MATLAB is typically very flexible in terms of ways in which options are defined, and you should consult the documentation on the myriads of ways of specifying options for, e.g., a plot. For example, one can specify plot color using the following:

```
>> plot(x,y,'color','green');
```

Well, this is what we have for the **plot** command. The plot command has very extensive documentation, listing its numerous properties and customizations.

Something has to be said for plotting complex numbers: the real and imaginary parts are only plotted if **plot** takes a single input array that happens to contain complex values. If you supply more than one array, imaginary values of all of the input arrays are all ignored. Then again, sometimes it's not such a bad thing:

```
x = [-2:.001:2];
y = (sqrt(cos(x)).*cos(200*x)+sqrt(abs(x))-0.7).*(4-x.*x).^0.01;
plot(x,y);
Warning: Imaginary parts of complex X
and/or Y arguments ignored
```

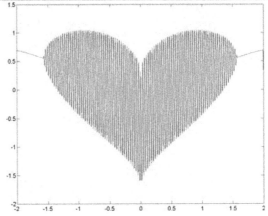

Figure 23: A plot of the function $f = \left(\sqrt{\cos x}\cos(200x) + \sqrt{|x|} - 0.7\right)(4 - x^2)^{0.01}$.
Imaginary values of y are completely ignored.

Multiple Plots from 2D Arrays

The `plot` function also lets us plot several sets of values at the same time. Naturally, this use of the function requires us to provide two-dimensional arrays of y values. Preparing data for such a plot is a bit more challenging, so let's take a step-by-step look at generating, for example, several Brownian motion paths. To do this, we'll be using the following formula:

$$W_{i+1} = W_i + Z\sqrt{dt} \text{ where } Z \sim \mathcal{N}(0,1) \text{ and } W_0 = 0$$

We begin by defining the number of paths to generate and the number of points in each of the paths. We also generate a range of time values and calculate dt , the size of one time increment:

```
pathCount = 6; % number of paths
pointCount = 500; % points per path
t = linspace(0,1,pointCount+1);
dt = t(2)-t(1);
```

So far, so good, right? Well, don't celebrate just yet. We now need to calculate the Brownian increments ($dW = Z\sqrt{dt}$), but remember that we need to multiply $\sqrt{dt}$ by each of the 6×500 values sampled from the Normal distribution. Luckily, as with most of MATLAB's functions, the function **randn** that generates Normally distributed values can take two parameters indicating the dimensions. This lets us calculate the increments:

```
dw = randn(pointCount,pathCount) * sqrt(dt);
```

Given that $\sqrt{dt}$ is a single value, there is no need for elementwise calculations; we now have a 6×500 array of increments and we're ready to calculate W_i. As we look at the recurrence relation we outlined at the beginning of the section, we realize that what we effectively have is a cumulative sum: at each W_i, we calculate the sum of all the increments up until that point (which we took care to preemptively multiply by $\sqrt{dt}$). Using MATLAB's **cumsum** function, we calculate the cumulative sums across the array of dW values, taking care to ensure the condition $W_0 = 0$:

```
w0 = zeros(1,pathCount);
w = cumsum([w0;dw]);
```

At last, we can take the array of W_i values and feed it to the plot function:

```
plot(w);
```

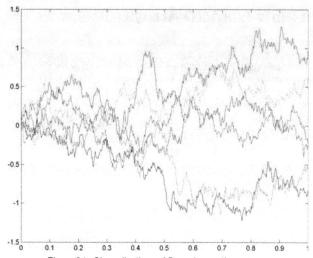

Figure 24: Six realizations of Brownian motion.

This image is what it's all been about: we've generated a 2D array of values such that it effectively contained several sets of realizations of Brownian motion. MATLAB then helped us draw each one as a separate line, and even added a splash of color.

Surface Plots

Phew, that was a tough one! At any rate, let's get back to plotting things. Another command that we used for surface rendering was called **surf**. Here's what its invocation from the command line would look like:

```
>> [x,y] = meshgrid(-10:0.5:10,-10:0.5:10);
>> z = sin(x) ./ cosh(y);
>> surf(z)
```

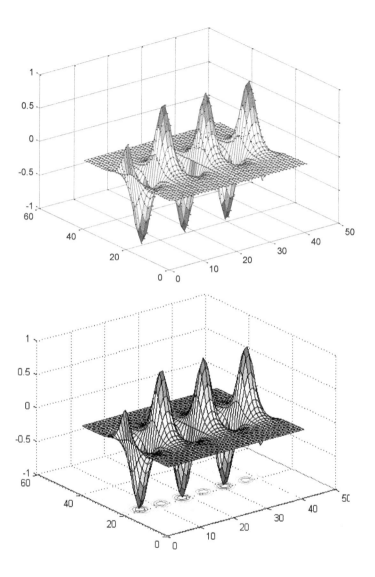

In the above case, it's as simple as calling **surf** with a single parameter. But let's say we wanted to customize it: by default, the command colors the highest z-values red and the lowest blue. What if we wanted the coloring along the x axis instead? In this case, we would need to call a more complete **surf** command—we provide x, y and z values and indicate explicitly that we want to use x for the color:

```
>> surf(x,y,z,x)
```

Note the color distribution:

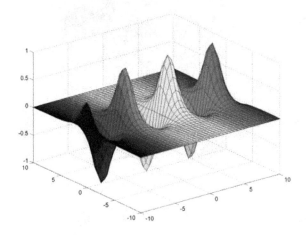

Figure 25: The function $f(x,y) = \frac{\sin x}{\cosh y}$ rendered with coloring along the x axis.

We could go on practically forever discussing the different plot types, but since space is limited, we leave it to the reader to investigate.

Table 1. Common Plot Types

Plot type	What it draws
plot, plotyy	Two-dimensional plot of data. The 'yy' variety renders the y axis on both left and right hand sides of the plot.

Plot type	What it draws
`semilogx,` `semilogy`	A plot with a logarithmic scale on either the x or y axis.
`loglog`	A plot with logarithmic scales on both the x and y axes.
`bar, barh`	Vertical and horizontal bar graph.
`area`	Area plot.
`pie`	Pie chart.
`hist`	A histogram.

The MATLAB Plot Gallery contains a particularly good selection of different plot types, and is worth checking out.

Figures and Multiple Plots

So you may have noticed that any time you make a new plot, you lose the existing one. What can we do about it? Well, first of all, you need to be aware of the `figure` command. This command creates an empty figure window, i.e. a window that you can render your plots in. You can actually invoke the command several times, creating more than one of these windows.

Say you have several figure windows. If you now invoke a command such as **plot**, it will render to the figure window that's currently in focus. But, if you render twice to the same figure window, you will lose the old image—unless, of course, you used the **hold on** command beforehand.

One thing I haven't mentioned is the idea of plot handles. Essentially, once you plot something to a figure window, you can change its properties post-hoc. For example, say you did a plot but forgot to set the color of the line. Luckily, there's a fix for this, because all graphic objects in MATLAB have handles (this is why MATLAB's graphics are called "Handle Graphics"). So what you can do is preserve a handle to the plot and then use the **set** command to adjust its property:

```
>> p = ezplot('x^3');
>> set(p,'color','red');
```

As you may have guessed, in addition to **set** there is a corresponding **get** function for reading properties.

In case you want to save a figure window as an image (e.g., PNG or PDF), you can use the **saveas** function. This function uses the current window handle (which MATLAB lets you access through a function called **gcf**) and the file format is actually inferred from the extension of the filename you specify. For example, to save a figure window as PNG (exactly what the author did while preparing this book's manuscript), we write **saveas(gcf, 'test.png')**.

Customizing Plots

Let's get back to our plot of the **sin** and **cos** functions and try to add some extra embellishments to our plot. The first thing you might want to do is add some labels to the coordinate axes (note that these don't go through the origin—we'll deal with this later).

```
>> xlabel('x');
>> ylabel('${\sin x}, {\cos x}$','interpreter','latex')
```

The first line is straightforward, but the second line is doing something else entirely. Essentially, for the y label, I decided to use LaTeX instead of plain text. As a result, I've had to use special notation and also had to tell MATLAB to use a LaTeX interpreter (once again, using the notation '*key*', '*value*' to specify options).

Next up, we want to add legend text for the different colored lines. Let's use LaTeX once again, but this time set the interpreter post-hoc:

```
>> l = legend('$\sin x$', '$\cos y$');
Warning: Unable to interpret TeX string
"$\sin x$"
Warning: Unable to interpret TeX string
"$\cos y$"
>> set(l,'interpreter','latex')
>> set(l,'location','north')
```

Note MATLAB's complaints about not being able to interpret a string—it expects a TeX string, whose syntax is slightly different to LaTeX string. After we set the right option, all is fixed. Also, we set the position of the legend box to **north**, meaning top-and-center of the figure window.

Finally, let's set the plot title:

```
>> title('sin and cos functions')
```

And, after all these customizations, here is the image we get:

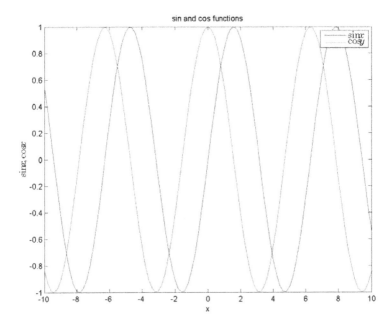

Figure 26: Functions $f(x) = \sin x$ and $f(x) = \cos x$ rendered with x and y labels, legend text, and title.

Subplots

The idea of subplots is to have several plots appear in a single figure window, but instead of overlapping each other, the subplots feature lets you put several plots side-by-side by effectively subdividing a single figure window into an M-by-N grid. This is best illustrated with an example. First of all, I create a new figure window, use the **subplot** function to create a plot in the first quadrant of a 2×2 window arrangement (these are supplied as function arguments), and then do a plot in that area.

```
>> figure
>> subplot(2,2,1)
>> ezplot('x^2')
```

Try it. I will not present the result here because it looks a bit silly to have an image with 75 percent whitespace. Instead, let's complete the other plots (with indices 2, 3, and 4) and then look at the result.

```
>> subplot(2,2,2)
>> ezplot('gamma(x)')
>> subplot(2,2,3)
>> ezsurf('sin(x)*cos(y)')
>> subplot(2,2,4)
>> ezplot3('sin(t)','cos(t)','t',[0,6*pi])
```

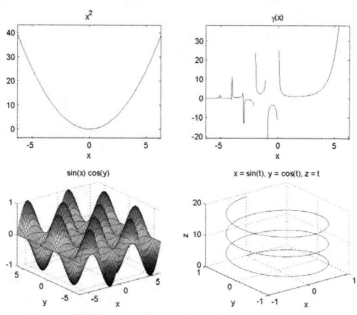

Figure 27: Four different subplots illustrating the functions $f(x) = x^2$, $f(x) = \Gamma(x)$, and $f(x,y) = \sin x \cos y$, and a parametric plot with $x = \sin t, y = \cos(t), z = t$ for $t = 0..6\pi$.

We have been a bit lazy in the above demo by using functions such as **ezplot** and **ezsurf**, which are part of the core MATLAB installation. This was done for the sake of brevity.

> **Note: You can have your subplot take up more than one cell in a grid of plots by specifying an array of cell positions to occupy. For example,**

$subplot(2,2,3:4)$ **will take up the whole bottom part of a 2×2 plot window.**

The tools provided by MATLAB let you manipulate each of the subplots (e.g., rotate or pan) individually. There are no hard constraints in terms of the number of subplots you can have within a single plot, and as soon as you exceed the dimension of the original plot grid, MATLAB repositions the existing subplot windows to accommodate the new structure.

Plot Editing in the Figure Window

Once we've rendered our graph, we can modify the graph either using the command window or by using the user interface of the Figure window itself. We can rotate and pan plots, add axes labels, legend text, and other things. These actions are available either from the toolbar or from the top-level menu of the figure window:

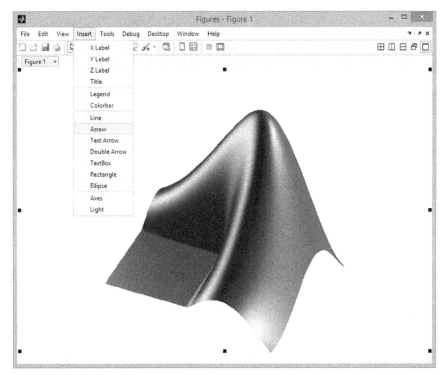

Figure 28: Editing a plot in the figure window.

Both the toolbar and the **Tools** menu let you customize the way that the figure looks; you can rotate the image, pan, zoom in and out, and a lot more.

There is one menu item I want to mention in particular: using **File | Generate Code**, we can generate a script file containing all the plot customizations that you applied using the UI. This is an excellent choice for demonstration scripts when you want to present a plot in just the right way.

Plotting Origin Axes

Every piece of software has its pain points, and MATLAB's pain point is its inability to automatically render the origin axes when plotting graphs. Instead, what you typically get on a graph is a set of edge markers rather than lines going through zero.

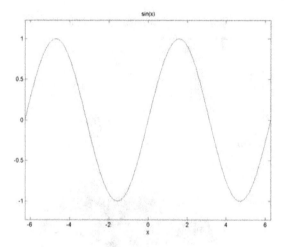

Figure 29: Graph of f(x)=sin(x) without axis lines.

One might think there is some easy solution to this problem, but unfortunately, there is not. So, what can we do about it? Well, the simplest solution is that you can turn on the grid:

```
>> grid on
```

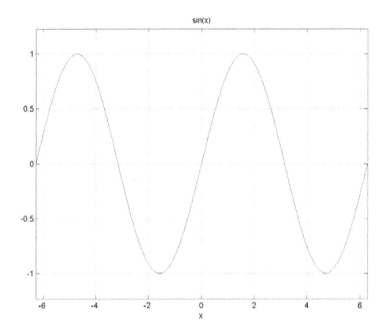

Figure 30: Function graph with the grid turned on.

The dotted, equally spaced grid lines are good indicators of where the graph lies, but this isn't the same as drawing axes lines, because there are too many lines, and it doesn't emphasize the lines going through zero.

Another option is to draw the lines yourself. You can get the figure limits from the **xlim** and **ylim** variables and then simply draw the lines through the origin:

```
>> xl = xlim;
>> yl = ylim;
>> line([0 0], yl ,'color','black')
>> line(xl, [0 0] ,'color','black')
```

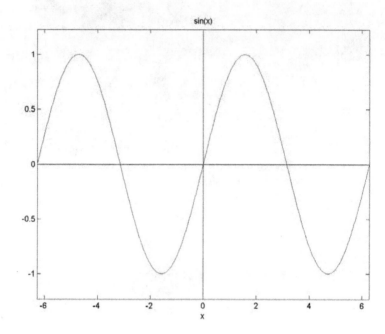

Figure 31: Axes lines rendered with the Line command.

There are no tick marks or arrowheads here; we get just the lines. Not to mention the fact that if you pan or rotate the view, you will get a broken-looking graph.

My advice is to use a third-party component. For example, I use a component called **oaxes** that renders the axes together with arrow heads and tick marks. This implementation also renders the Z axis if you need it, and it actually supports panning/rotating the graph. It is a bit slow to render, but it is the best solution we have.

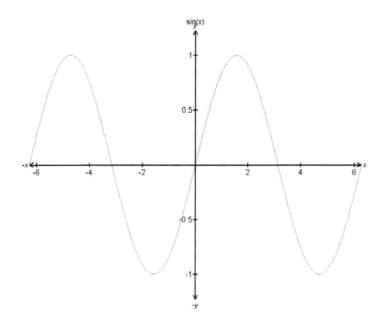

Figure 32: Axes lines rendered via the oaxes component.

To download oaxes (or some other solution), head over to MATLAB Central's File Exchange (FEX). Oaxes, like all other FEX submissions, is open-source software.

Image Processing

All graphs that we've plotted so far were meant to visualize data, but MATLAB also supports dedicated functions for interacting with images (and, by extension, movies).

In order to appreciate MATLAB's image processing capabilities, let's try loading the following image. To load an image, we can either use the big Import Data button or the **imread** function.

Figure 33: Our original image, taken at a café in Sigtuna, Sweden's oldest city.

Let's examine what we actually get as we load this image into MATLAB:

```
>> pic = imread('33.png');
>> whos pic
  Name         Size                Bytes  Class     Attributes

  pic       1772x1181x3          6278196  uint8
```

So the image got converted into a 1772 x 1181 x 3 array of uint unit values. You can already guess that the first two dimensions correspond to the width and height of the image and the third dimension is used to contain the red, green, and blue values respectively. The class **uint8** basically means a single-byte (8-bit) integer value having a range 0..255.

To get MATLAB to render this (or any other) image, we can simply write **image(pic)**. But let's manipulate it first. For example, we can invert the image and save it with:

```
>> pic2 = 255 - pic;
>> imwrite(pic2,'34.png')
```

Figure 34: The inverted image.

Of course, in addition to being able to change the pixel value ourselves, MATLAB also provides a wealth of functions for manipulating images. It has functions for geometric transformations, image enhancement, analysis, and plenty of other things that are too advanced for non-professionals.

Chapter 7 Object-Oriented Programming

So far, all we've seen in MATLAB is a fairly procedural style of programming where statements get executed in the order they are defined. To add structure and support larger, more complicated scripts, MATLAB supports the notion of object-oriented programming. This mechanism allows for clear organization of properties and behavioral aspects of different concepts.

Classes

Object-Oriented Programming (OOP) is a way of modeling real-world concepts as objects. In our example, we're going to create a model of a bank account. Strictly speaking, we could continue using structures, so in MATLAB we could for example write `account.balance = 0`, and this would automatically create a structure with an appropriate field. However, the problem with this approach is that we may subsequently want to withdraw or deposit money on the account or, for example, get notifications when we go below our balance. A structure does not provide a mechanism for us to do this right in its own definition.

We need a different way of modeling an account, and for this we can define a class of its own called `Account` that will reside in a script file called **Account.m**—note that MATLAB insists on a 1-to-1 correspondence between the name of the file and the name of the class or function that the file contains. Classes are defined using the `classdef` keyword.

Before we start writing our class, I would like to make a critical distinction between two types of classes—handle and value classes.

Value classes behave similarly to structures and ordinary types of variables, meaning that they are essentially data containers, and any time you store such a class somewhere, you essentially perform a full copy of its data, which might not be very efficient if the class is large.

The other type of data is handle classes. These are referenced via handles, which are equivalent to pointers or references in other programming languages. A single handle class instance can be referenced by more than one object or function, and all of these would point to just one object, so the memory used by the data is not duplicated (unlike the case of value classes). Each data item is only stored once in memory.

Handle classes, as you'll see in a moment, inherit from the correspondingly named **handle** class. Any MATLAB class that inherits another class also inherits its type (value or handle). Inheritance is optional: a class that does not inherit another class is a value class; a class that directly or indirectly inherits the handle class is a handle class.

Our class will be a handle class:

```
classdef Account < handle
```

```
end
```

The operator < is, in this case, used to indicate inheritance. It is entirely optional; a class may have no inheritors at all.

Having created the account (and saved the file, of course), we can now start using it:

```
>> a = Account

a =
  Account with no properties
```

If we use our trusty **whos** command, we will get the following information about our **Account** instance:

```
>> whos a

  Name      Size            Bytes  Class      Attributes
  a         1x1               112  Account
```

The class of the variable is, predictably, **Account**. Once again, its size is 1×1—it's quite obviously an array, so we could write **a(2)** = **Account** and get another array element, also of type **Account**. In fact, we can initialize a whole array of **Account** objects with the following:

```
>> b(1:5) = Account

b =
  1x5 Account array with no properties
```

Properties

A bank account typically has a balance, so let us create the corresponding property of the **Account** class. Properties are defined in a **properties** block:

```
classdef Account < handle
  properties
    Balance = 0
  end
end
```

The above code gives **Account** a property called **Balance**, and since bank accounts are typically empty by default, we initialize its value to 0 (zero).

Note: After you modify the structure of a class, you cannot rely on MATLAB to upgrade your class instances to the new definitions. This means that in order to use the updated definition you need to call the `clear` command and then recreate the variables again. In many cases even this is not enough, and the only solution is to restart MATLAB.

At any rate, having created an instance of the **Account** class, we can now read and write its balance:

```
>> a.Balance = 100

a =
  Account with properties:
    Balance: 100

>> disp(a.Balance)
    100
```

Overall, properties feel very much like structure fields, don't they? So far there doesn't seem to be much difference between the two constructs. But one thing you can implement with properties is encapsulation.

Encapsulation lets you control who can access a class member, and who cannot. In the case of properties, you can use the **GetAccess** and **SetAccess** attributes (or the joint `Access` specifier) on a property to define whether the properties are accessible to everyone (public) or just to the class they're defined in (private).

Attributes

Options defined right after the block keyword are called attributes. They are used to customize the behavior of all the members with the block.

```
classdef Account
  properties (SetAccess = private) % GetAccess is public
    Risk
  end
  properties (Access = private)
    ID
  end
end
```

Here are the consequences of trying to use these properties in the Command Window:

```
>> m = MyClass

m =
  MyClass with properties:
    alpha: []
```

```
>> m.alpha

ans =
     []

>> m.alpha = 23
You cannot set the read-only property 'alpha'
of MyClass.

>> m.beta = 91
You cannot set the 'beta' property of MyClass.
```

Methods

Now that we have a Balance property for our Account, what we want is to be able to deposit and withdraw money from the account. These are behaviors of the account, and they can be modeled using methods. For this, we need a **methods** block.

```
classdef Account < handle
  methods
  end
  % other class members omitted
End
```

Now, what is a method, exactly? Well, it is simply a function (and we've already met functions) that can access other elements (i.e. properties and methods) of the class in which it is contained. So let's make a method for depositing money into the account:

```
methods
  function deposit(obj,amount)
    obj.Balance = obj.Balance + amount;
  end
end
```

This is somewhat similar to a typical function declaration, but what is **obj**? Well, the first parameter to a method is actually a reference to the containing class. So the only way we can refer to the **Balance** property is through this parameter. Don't worry though—you will never have to provide the value explicitly, so if you want to deposit money to the account, you simply need to write:

```
>> a.deposit(100)
>> a

a =
  Account with properties:
    Balance: 100
```

Please note that in addition to calling the **deposit()** method as **a.deposit(100)**, it is also possible to invoke it as **deposit(a, 100)**—the end result of these two calls is the same.

How about withdrawing money from the account? Similar idea here, except that we don't want to let the account user withdraw more than they've actually got:

```
function withdraw(obj,amount)
  if (amount <= obj.Balance)
    obj.Balance = obj.Balance - amount;
  else
    disp('insufficient funds')
  end
end
```

And here are some attempts to withdraw money from the account:

```
>> a.withdraw(50)
>> a.Balance

ans =
    50

>> a.withdraw(1000)
insufficient funds
```

Constructors

It is somewhat tedious to have to first create an empty **Account** and then initialize it with a starting balance. To collapse this process to one line we can define a constructor. A constructor is a special method called when you initialize the object. Here's how you define one:

```
function obj = Account(startingBalance)
  obj.Balance = startingBalance;
end
```

A constructor is special: it has the same name as the containing class, and instead of taking **obj** (or whatever you decide to call the object reference) as a parameter, it actually returns it instead. And here's how you can use it:

```
>> a = Account(30)

a =

  Account with properties:
```

```
Balance: 30
```

Any time you call a constructor, a new, separate object is created. When you assign a variable to a property of one instance of a class, other instances are not affected:

```
>> a = Account(30);
>> b = Account(10);
>> c = a;
>> c.Balance = 15;
>> a.Balance

ans =
    15

>> b.Balance

ans =
    10
```

Events

Let us suppose that, in the system we are modeling, we've also got a bank manager who happens to be very interested in cases when people try to withdraw more money than they have. The manager can, for example, offer overdraft facilities to such persons.

To implement this functionality, we will create a new class called **BankManager**. The bank manager won't have any properties, only a method for offering overdrafts. Also, since there is only one bank manager in our system, we can define its methods as **Static**, which means that you don't even have to create any instances of **BankManager** for the method to fire!

```
classdef BankManager
  methods (Static)
    function OfferOverdraft()
      disp('Would you like an overdraft?')
    end
  end
end
```

As you can see, the function doesn't even have an **obj** parameter because it doesn't require an instance of the surrounding class. Now, the idea is that the bank manager is somehow able to watch a particular account:

```
function Watch(account)
  % nothing here (yet)
end
```

But of course we need the bank account to be able to notify everyone that an "insufficient funds" event occurs. And the way it does it is by declaring an events block and defining an event:

```
Events
  InsufficientFunds
end
methods
  function withdraw(obj,amount)
    if (amount <= obj.Balance)
      obj.Balance = obj.Balance - amount;
    else
      notify(obj,'InsufficientFunds');
    end
  end
% other class members omitted
End
```

In the above, we declare an event called **InsufficientFunds** and then, inside the **Withdraw** method, we explicitly fire the event using the **notify** function, letting all the subscribers know that someone is out of funds.

Now we can jump back to the **BankManager** class and complete the **Watch** method:

```
function Watch(account)
  addlistener(account,'InsufficientFunds', ...
    @(sourceHandle,eventData) BankManager.OfferOverdraft());
End
```

Explanations are definitely in order here. First of all, just as **notify** is a special function for firing an event and notifying all subscribers, **addlistener** is a function for subscribing to the event. This function takes as parameters the object to observe and the name of the event to subscribe to, as well as an anonymous function that defines how exactly we want to handle the event. The function parameters contain information about event and where the event came from.

And here is how it can all be used:

```
>> a = Account(5);
>> BankManager.Watch(a)
>> a.withdraw(10)
Would you like an overdraft?
```

Note that calls to **BankManager**'s methods happen without instance variables (such as **obj**), but rather through the class name. This is, once again, due to the fact that its functions are all static and do not require an object instance.

Inheritance

It's time to discuss one of the central features of object-oriented programming: inheritance. Inheritance basically allows classes to inherit, or to magically acquire, methods or properties of another class. We've already done this once by inheriting the **Account** class from handle, and we're now going to do this once again.

This time, we're going to have another kind of account called **SmartAccount**, which is going to inherit from **Account** and provide additional functionality. Specifically, we add the ability to close the account:

```
classdef SmartAccount < Account
   methods
     function Close(obj)
        obj.Withdraw(obj.Balance);
        disp('account closed');
     end
   end
end
```

As you can see, inheritance is defined by writing **< Account** just after the class definition. This means that **SmartAccount** automatically acquires the property **Balance**, the methods **Withdraw** and **Deposit**, and the event **InsufficientFunds**. It also becomes a handle class, since that's what its parent class inherits from. Plus, it gets a method, **Close**, which is entirely its own:

```
>> a = SmartAccount;
>> BankManager.Watch(a);
>> a.Deposit(50);
>> a.Withdraw(75);
Would you like an overdraft?
>> a.Balance
ans =
    50
>> a.Close();
account closed
>> a.Balance
ans =
    0
```

One interesting thing that many modern programming languages are missing is MATLAB's ability for a class to have more than one parent (i.e. to inherit from more than one class). That's right—MATLAB has multiple inheritance, and despite the potential dangers in the approach, it's there if you need it!

Enumerations

Let's say that I want to prevent anyone from trying to close an already closed **SmartAccount**. To accomplish this, I want to track the state of the account (opened or closed). The account can be in one of several discrete states, and discrete value collections can be defined in a so-called enumeration class. This is rather simple—all we need is an ordinary class definition with a special **enumeration** block containing all the possible states:

```
classdef AccountState
  enumeration
    Open, Closed
  end
end
```

Now we can jump back to the **SmartAccount** class and add an additional property of type **AccountState**. Let us assume that, by default, an account is in the **Open** state:

```
classdef SmartAccount < Account
  properties
    State = AccountState.Open
  end
  methods
    function Close(obj)
      obj.Withdraw(obj.Balance);
      disp('account closed');
    end
  end
end
```

Now we need to actually check and alter state when closing the account. This is rather simple:

```
function Close(obj)
  if obj.State == AccountState.Closed
    error('account already closed.');
  else
    obj.Withdraw(obj.Balance);
    disp('account closed');
    obj.State = AccountState.Closed;
  end
end
```

And that's it! Now, trying to close the account twice gives us the following:

```
>> a = SmartAccount;
>> a.Close();
account closed
>> a.Close();
account already closed.
```

Chapter 8 A Mathematical Smörgåsbord

We have spent most of this book discussing the facilities MATLAB provides; now let's take a look at a few hands-on examples. After all, scripts and plots and OOP are all very nice, but sometimes you just want to calculate something, and it is great to know in advance what function to call.

Elementary Math

No, really, I'm not going to reiterate primary school material. What I will talk about are some of the most basic facilities that are implemented via functions.

Let's start with a simple fact: every operator, be it * or .^ or the matrix \ operator, has a correspondingly named function. For example, + can be invoked as

```
>> plus(i,j)

ans =
   0.0000 + 2.0000i
```

These notations are of little use to us (who would want to be using functions instead of operators?) except in cases where we want to use them as function handles, or when we want to implement (overload) it for our classes. For example, say you have a class called Size and you want to support two sizes being added together. In this case, you define your class like this:

```
classdef Size < handle
  properties
    w = 0
    h = 0
  end
  methods
    function obj = Size(ww,hh)
      obj.w = ww;
      obj.h = hh;
    end
    function obj = plus(a,b)
      obj = Size(a.w + b.w, a.h + b.h);
    end
  end
end
```

The **plus** function takes care of the operator calls, and here's how you would use it:

```
>> s1 = Size(2,3);
```

```
>> s2 = Size(20,30);
>> s1+s2

ans =

  Size with properties:

    w: 22
    h: 33
```

Next up, we have various cumulative calculation functions. For example, **sum** and **prod** calculate the sum or product of all the elements in an array (these functions generally do not care about array dimensions—they treat all arrays as flattened). In addition to **cumsum** (cumulative sum) that we've already seen, there is a corresponding **cumprod** (cumulative product) function.

```
>> x = [1 2 3 4];
>> sum(x),prod(x)

ans =
    10


ans =
    24

>> cumsum(x),cumprod(x)

ans =
    1    3    6    10

ans =
    1    2    6    24
```

There is also a function called **diff** that calculates the differences between adjacent elements in an array. One of its uses is to calculate the "delta" value of an array initialized with **linspace**:

```
>> z = linspace(0,1,101);
>> dz = diff(z(1:2))

dz =

    0.0100
```

Lastly, we have functions for calculating the floor and ceiling of a number—these are **floor** and **ceil**, respectively. Also, we have the **round** function that rounds to the nearest integer, and **fix**, which rounds towards zero:

```
>> y=-5.55;
>> [floor(y) ceil(y) round(y) fix(y)]

ans =
    -6    -5    -6    -5
```

Finally, **mod** does modulo division (MATLAB hijacked the % operator for comments, unfortunately) and **rem** calculates the remainder of division. These are identical for positive values but yield different results for negative ones:

```
>> [mod(11,3),rem(11,3);mod(-11,3),rem(-11,3)]

ans =

     2     2
     1    -2
```

Trigonometry, Exponents, and Logs

Life wouldn't be fun without trigonometry, would it? As one would expect, MATLAB comes with support for all the common trig functions and their hyperbolic variations. Bizarrely, each function exists in two variations: an ordinary function that takes its arguments in radians, and the same function postfixed with **-d** (e.g., **cosd**) that takes degrees. Also, inverse functions are prefixed with a rather than **arc**, so the inverse cotangent would be **acot**.

The only function of note is **hypot**, which calculates the square root of the sum of squares (or the hypotenuse of a triangle).

```
>> hypot(3,4)

ans =
     5
```

Moving on, we have the fairly obvious **exp** (calculates $e^{\wedge}x$, note there is no "e" constant in MATLAB), **log** (the natural logarithm), and **sqrt** ($\sqrt{x}$). **log10** calculates the base 10 logarithm. There are also more obscure functions to calculate logarithms and exponents for small values of x as well as versions of **exp/log/sqrt** prefixed with **real-** that throw exceptions on negative input:

```
>> realsqrt(-1)
Error using realsqrt
```

```
Realsqrt produced complex result.
```

Complex Numbers

The support for complex numbers is built into MATLAB, and you get the **i/j** constants (functions, really, but you get the idea) for defining and manipulating complex values. In addition to ordinary arithmetic, you can calculate the **real** and **imag** (imaginary) parts of complex numbers, the complex **conj** (conjugate) and a few other, less exciting things.

```
>> u = 2+3i;
>> [real(u) imag(u) conj(u)]

ans =
   2.0000 + 0.0000i   3.0000 + 0.0000i   2.0000 - 3.0000i
```

Notice how the result of **real** is still a complex number.

Note that there is a difference between calling **x'** and **transpose(x)** on a matrix that has complex values: the first performs a conjugate transpose, the second a non-conjugate one:

```
>> a = sqrt(-magic(2))
a =
   0.0000 + 1.0000i   0.0000 + 1.7321i
   0.0000 + 2.0000i   0.0000 + 1.4142i

>> a'
ans =
   0.0000 - 1.0000i   0.0000 - 2.0000i
   0.0000 - 1.7321i   0.0000 - 1.4142i

>> transpose(a)
ans =

   0.0000 + 1.0000i   0.0000 + 2.0000i
   0.0000 + 1.7321i   0.0000 + 1.4142i
```

Special Functions

While MATLAB doesn't give you every single special function under the sun, it does give you the popular ones such as **Beta**, **Gamma**, a variety of **Bessel** functions, the **Error** function, and its complementary functions such as the **Legendre** function.

Also, MATLAB isn't shy in using special functions in its own results when it cannot derive something. For example, using the Symbolic Toolbox to calculate $\int \blacksquare x^\wedge n \ e^\wedge x$ we get:

```
>> int(x^n*exp(x),x)
ans =
(x^n*igamma(n + 1, -x))/(-x)^n
```

Of course, it would be very surprising if we actually got an analytic solution for the above integral!

Discrete Math

As we've mentioned in our discussion on basic syntax, MATLAB has hijacked the ! operator to send calls to the underlying operating system. This unfortunately prevents us from being able to use ! for factorials—instead MATLAB gives us the **factorial** function. Oh, and there is no double factorial or subfactorial support, which can be a problem if you want to solve that famous "2008" problem.

Discrete math functions let you calculate lots of independent things, like the greatest common divisor and least common multiple (**gcd** and **lcm** respectively), prime values such as the lowest prime less or equal to a value (**primes**), or all the prime factors of a number (**factor**).

Incidentally, you'll sometimes see toolboxes reuse (overload) existing functions for their own, nefarious ends. The **factor** function is a good example:

```
>> syms a b
>> factor(a*x*x+b*x)

ans =
x*(b + a*x)
```

Test Matrices

MATLAB has lots of different functions for generating various matrices useful for testing or demonstrations. We've already used the magic square matrix to show sorting, but there are lots of other matrices such as the Hilbert, Hadamard, Toeplitz, Hankel, and other matrices.

In addition to these, there is also a **gallery** function that has even more sample matrices (use **help gallery** to get a listing). For example, to generate a 5 × 5 matrix filled with zeros or ones, you can write:

```
>> gallery('rando',5)
```

The "2008" Problem

If you enjoy a math challenge, here's a tough one for you: you're given 13 zeros (yes, zeros, as in **zeros(13,1)**). Use these zeroes and various mathematical operations to perform a calculation that will result in the value 2008.

(Just in case you are wondering, 2008 is a number that was deliberately chosen to make the solution to this problem non-trivial.)

Bonus round: try getting 2008 with less than 13 zeros.

Some solutions to this problem are provided at the end of this chapter.

```
ans =

     1     0     0     1     0
     0     1     1     1     0
     0     0     1     0     0
     0     0     1     1     0
     1     0     0     0     0
```

Interpolation

MATLAB supports several types of interpolation. Let's look at 1D interpolation first—this requires juts a single list of values. The **spline** function, for instance, lets us perform cubic interpolation, which lets us "fill in the dots" on an incomplete data set:

```
>> x = linspace(0,3*pi,11);
>> y = sin(x) ./ x;
>> x2 = linspace(0,3*pi,101);
>> y2 = spline(x,y,x2);
Warning: Columns of data containing NaN values have been ignored during
interpolation.
> In interp1>Interp1DStripNaN at 239
  In interp1 at 176
>> plot(x,y,'xr',x2,y2)
```

And here's the plot with x marks indicating the original values, and the line indicating the interpolated spline:

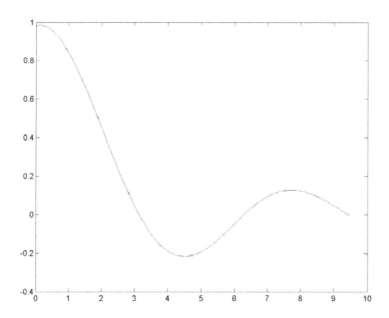

Figure 35: Original values and the interpolated spline.

In fact, the **spline** function is a specialization of the **interp1** function with a 'spline' parameter. For 2D and 3D data we simply have **interp2** and **interp3** respectively. To illustrate 3D interpolation, let's use the **flow** function to generate a coarse approximation of fluid flow and then interpolate over a finer mesh:

```
[x,y,z,v] = flow(10);
[xi,yi,zi] = meshgrid(0.1:.2:10,-4:.2:4,-4:.2:4);
vi = interp3(x,y,z,v,xi,yi,zi);
slice(xi,yi,zi,vi,[6 9.5],2,[-2 .2])
shading('flat')
```

To render the image shown below, we used the **slice** function to effectively take and show slices out of a volumetric plot:

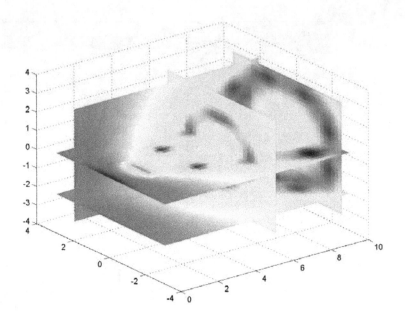

Figure 36: Slice plot of an interpolated flow model.

Incidentally, it's worth mentioning that in addition to `meshgrid`, which works in 2D and 3D space, there is also a corresponding `ngrid` function that works in N-D space. Its operation is very similar to `meshgrid`: you simply provide the coordinate values for however many dimensions you have and get the corresponding set of arrays.

Optimization

MATLAB supports typical optimization problems: minimizing or maximizing single- or multivariate functions and solving constraint problems. Optimization is a very big topic, so we'll just look at a few examples, and you can consult the MATLAB documentation and relevant texts on all the scary details of various optimization problems.

Consider the function $f(x) = \frac{\sin x}{e^x}$

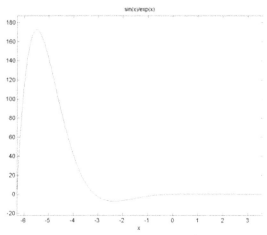

Figure 37: A plot of the function $f(x) = \frac{\sin x}{e^x}$.

To locate the local minimum in the range (-4, 0) we need, first of all, to define the function to search over—MATLAB's support for function literals comes in handy here. Then, we use the **fminbnd** function to find the minimum within the specified bounds:

```
>> f = @(x) sin(x)/exp(x)

f =

    @(x)sin(x)/exp(x)

>> fminbnd(f,-4,0)

ans =

        -2.3561989868868
```

There is no corresponding maximizing function: if you need the maximum of $f(x)$, simply calculate the mimimum of $-f(x)$.

In addition to supporting functions of one variable, MATLAB also supports searching for minimums of functions of many variables. For instance, let us suppose that you want to find the maximum of $f(x_1, x_2) = x_1 e^{-x_1^2 - x_2^2}$, which looks like this:

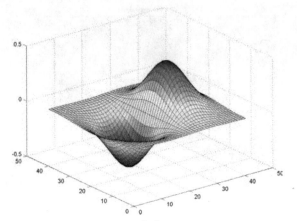

Figure 38: Surface plot of the function $f(x_1, x_2) = x_1 e^{-x_1^2 - x_2^2}$. A particularly good-looking plot that MATLAB documentation really likes to show off.

We can instruct MATLAB to search for a minimum starting somewhere in the (10, 20) range:

```
>> f = @(x) x(1)*exp(-x(1)^2-x(2)^2);
>> fminsearch(f,[10 20])

ans =
              11.3125              25.875
```

Note that, unlike the bounded **fminbnd**, **fminsearch** performs unconstrained optimization.

Let's move on. The **fzero** function attempts to locate a root of one equation with one variable. For example, given the following function:

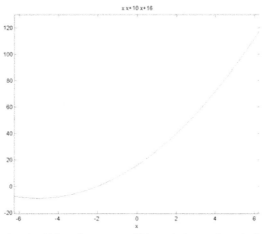

Figure 39: A plot of the function $f(x) = x^2 + 10x + 16$. This quadratic equation actually has two roots, but we constrained the range in this chart, so you only see one.

We can locate the root by making the assumption that it lies somewhere in the (-6, 6) range:

```
>> f = @(x) x*x+10*x+16;
>> options = optimset('Display','iter');
>> fzero(f,[-6 6],options)

Func-count     x              f(x)            Procedure
   2          -6             -8              initial
   3          -5.2           -8.96           interpolation
   4          -5.2           -8.96           bisection
   5          -3.47692       -6.68024        interpolation
   6          -1.53846        2.98225        bisection
   7          -2.13675       -0.801812       interpolation
   8          -2.00998       -0.0597757      interpolation
   9          -1.99997        0.000194854    interpolation
  10          -2             -3.24619e-07    interpolation
  11          -2             -1.75504e-12    interpolation
  12          -2              0              interpolation

Zero found in the interval [-6, 6]

ans =

    -2
```

We have deliberately turned on verbose output options for the above call so as to show you the iterative process. Without the extra setting, the **fzero** call just gives you the final result.

MATLAB supports a few more optimization algorithms, but a lot more fun can be had with the Optimization Toolbox (for local optimizations) and the Global Optimization Toolbox.

Numerical Integration and Differential Equations

First and foremost, if you want **symbolic** differentiation or integration (i.e., analytical solutions rather than numeric ones), you need the Symbolic Math Toolbox, because MATLAB doesn't include this functionality by default. What MATLAB does give you is the ability to perform numerical integration and differentiation as well as methods for solving ordinary (ODE) and partial (PDE) differential equations.

Let's start with numeric integration. This is done using the `integral` function, and requires the function itself as well as the integration limits:

```
>> f = @(x) exp(-x.^2);
>> integral(f,0,1)

ans =
         0.746824132812427
```

 Note: Can you see anything unusual about this code sample? That's right— when working with numerical methods, your x value might be an array— ergo, we use the elementwise operator (x.^2). Had we used an ordinary exponentiation, we would get a rather cryptic error.

Double and triple integrals are evaluated with `integral2` and `integral3`, respectively. MATLAB also comes with support for a variety of numerical integration methods such as Trapezoidal (`trapz`) and Simpson (`quad`).

Now, let's move on to the fun stuff: solving ODEs (ordinary differential equations). MATLAB comes with several functions all prefixed with `ode-` followed by numbers and letters, such as `ode15i` and `ode23tb`. These are used to distinguish whether the equation to be solved is *stiff* or *nonstiff*, and what method (low order, medium order, etc.) is used to solve the equation.

For example, let's solve the equation:

$$y' = \frac{-ty}{\sqrt{2 - y^2}}$$

with initial conditions $y(0) = 1, t \in [0,5]$. For this, we first define our function:

```
>> f = @(t,y) -t*y/sqrt(2-y^2);
```

We then use **ode45** (nonstiff, medium order method) to solve the equation and plot the results:

```
>> [tt ff] = ode45(f,[0 5],1);
>> plot(tt,ff)
>> grid on
```

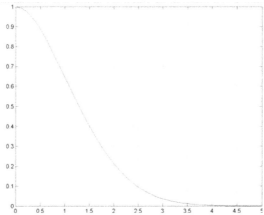

Figure 40: A plot of the solution to our differential equation.

The PDE solver that comes with MATLAB supports 1D parabolic-elliptic PDEs with initial-boundary values. The function **pdepe** is used to solve the equation, and **pdeval** evaluates the numerical solution using **pdepe**'s output. Additional PDE support is provided by functions in the Partial Differential Equation Toolbox.

Fourier Analysis and Filtering

In the realm of Fourier analysis the key operation is, of course, the Fast Fourier Transform function **fft** as well as its 2D and N-D variants (**fft2** and **fftn**) and their inverse transforms (**ifft**, **ifft2** and **ifftn** respectively).

As is custom, we illustrate FFT by first creating some data that includes both oscillations as well as noise:

```
fs = 1000;
t = 1/fs;
l = 1000;
```

```
t = (0:1-1)*t;
x = 0.6*sin(2*pi*50*t) + sin(2*pi*120*t);
y = x + 2*randn(size(t));
```

We now convert to the frequency domain and apply FFT to get the discrete Fourier transform of the noisy signal:

```
n = 2^nextpow2(1);
yy = fft(y,n)/1;
f = fs/2*linspace(0,1,n/2+1);
```

In the above, **nextpow2** gets us the next power of 2 of a variable. Having performed the transform, we can now plot the spectrum:

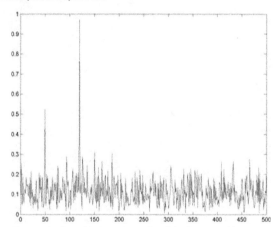

Figure 41: One-sided spectrum plot of the function $y(t)$.

And there you have it—two clear peaks at 50 and 120. Of course, thanks to the noise, we don't get the exact amplitudes, but then life isn't perfect either.

So let's now talk about filtering. MATLAB has functions for 1D and 2D digital filtering, 2D and N-D convolutions, and a few other things besides. Filtering, which in the 1D case is done with the **filter** function, is rather interesting. Its signature takes three parameters: the first two are the numerator and denominator coefficient vectors, and last one is the data to filter.

The filter function is useful for lots of things. For example, let's generate a random path and then plot the simple moving average of a few periods of data:

```
pointCount = 500;
t = linspace(0,1,pointCount+1);
dt=diff(t(1:2));
dw=randn(pointCount,1)*sqrt(dt);
w = cumsum([0;dw]);
```

```
periods = 30;
maData = filter(ones(1,periods)/periods,1,w);
plot(t,[w maData])
```

And here is the end result:

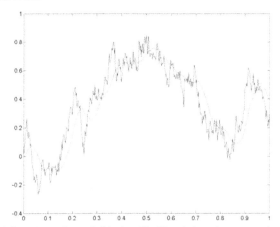

Figure 42: A Brownian motion path (blue) and its 30-period moving average (green).

 Note: The author of this manuscript makes no claims whatsoever as to the effectiveness of technical analysis techniques (such as use of moving averages) for purposes of financial analysis.

It's virtually impossible to cover every feature of MATLAB in a single book, so we'll stop here. It is a *Succinctly* title, after all.

The "2008" Problem

As promised, here's the solution to the problem presented earlier. First, a reminder: you are given thirteen zeros (0 0 0 0 0 0 0 0 0 0 0 0 0) and you need to use these zeros with some mathematical operations to arrive at a value of 2008.

The trick here is to use the factorial function and the fact that 0! = 1 to make some real numbers. The solution can then be acquired from adding up several 0! terms and taking their factorial so, for example

$$2008 = \frac{(3! + 1)!}{2} - 2^{3^2}$$

The use of double factorials allows for even shorter solutions. For example,

$$2008 = (3^* - 3! - 1)(3^* + 1) - 1$$

where $3^* = (3!)!! = 48$. Then there are subfactorials and lots of other tricks to reduce the number of required zeros to a minimum. See if you can find some shorter solutions.

In Closing

Thanks for reading the book! We have attempted to provide the readers with a comprehensive overview of MATLAB as a language and platform. The sum of domain knowledge that MATLAB possesses is enough to fill hundreds of books, and many of its facilities require a very good understanding of mathematics and other related disciplines.

To learn more about MATLAB, feel free to consult the built-in documentation as well as a great many books that other authors have published on the topic. You can also find plenty of information on the following sites:

- MATLAB Central: http://www.mathworks.com/matlabcentral/
- MathWorks Blogs: http://blogs.mathworks.com/
- MATLAB on StackOverflow: http://stackoverflow.com/questions/tagged/matlab

Good luck!